FRAGMENTS OF WAR
Stories from Survivors of World War II

by Joyce Hibbert
with a Foreword by Earle Birney

Dundurn Press
Toronto London
1985

Editor: Bernice Lever
Design and Production: Green Graphics
Typesetting, printing and binding:
The Coach House Press, Toronto

The Publication of this book was made possible by support
from several sources. The author and publisher wish to ack-
nowledge the generous assistance and ongoing support of the
Canada Council and the Ontario Arts Council.

J. Kirk Howard, Publisher

Dundurn Press Limited
P.O. Box 245, Station F
Toronto, Canada, M4Y 2L5

Canadian Cataloguing in Publication.

Hibbert, Joyce, 1923-
    Fragments of war: stories from survivors of World War II.

ISBN 0-919670-95-4 (bound). – ISBN 0-919670-94-6 (pbk.)

1. World, War, 1939-1945 – Personal narratives, Canadian.
2. Canada. Armed Forces – Biography. I. Title.

D811.A2H52 1985   940.54'81'71   C85-099331-8

British Cataloguing in Publication.

    Fragments of war: stories from survivors of World War II.
    1. World War, 1939-1945
    I. Hibbert, Joyce
    940.53   D743

ISBN 0-919760-95-4
ISBN 0-919760-94-6 Pbk

In Memory of those who did not survive the hazards of WWII

A conference of senior officers at First Canadian Headquarters,
Amblie, France, 4 August 1944, (left to right) Lieutenant General
H.D.G. Crerar, Air Marshall A.M. Coningham, General Sir Bernard
Montgomery, and Air Chief Marshall, Sir T.L. Leigh-Mallory.

Contents

Foreword

These memories of more than thirty Canadians separately caught up in the struggle against European fascism and its allies disprove Walt Whitman's sceptical dictum that "the real war will never get in the books". Certainly a remarkable mosaic of the incredibly varied realities of World War Two, as experienced by young Canadians, is recreated here with matter-of-fact clarity and unpretentious vividness. These chroniclers do not evade either the horrors or the grotesque comedies, the boredoms or the terrors.

Here, at the war's start, is an English woman emigrating to Canada, being chucked into a small lifeboat from the torpedoed *Athenia* on top of seventy other civilians heaped and vomiting on each other (except for one already dead).

Here is a Vancouver naval volunteer merely watching in dumb excitement and frustration, from his corvette in the Channel (as I did from a nearby shore), the aerial armada of D-Day roaring overhead to France. And there is the lone survivor from a bomber, blasted from the skies into three years of prison camps, enduring serious but untreatred injuries, Gestapo interrogations, starvation fare, forced marches and the daily expectation of being shot. That was a McGill student who endured to finish his courses and practice his profession.

An 18-year-old from New Brunswick signed up with the Royal Rifles just in time to fight and be captured in Hong Kong. He suffered four years of lethal slavery in Japanese hands, and then returned to Canada.

And there is a wonderfully lively Nursing Sister here from Montreal who served in Casualty Clearing Stations in many dangerous scenes. She is perhaps my favorite because among her many patients in the V-2 days around Nijmegen (when I was there) was a cheerful screwball who had been nicked in the butt. He could well have been my young friend of those vanished days, Pte. Thos. L. (Topsy) Turvey.

Earle Birney

Preface

Four decades have passed, and yet for many who were present on the massive revolving stage of an all-out world war, memories of that time remain vivid and compelling.

These stories have been gathered together to illustrate how a varied cross-section of Canadians met the main challenge of their youth. Most of those featured were volunteers who enlisted in Canada; others were caught up in the struggle against Fascism elsewhere and chose to become Canadians shortly after hostilities ceased.

Death and its grim retinue of terror, suffering, and imprisonment lurked in all theatres of conflict and took their inestimable toll. Although not always centre stage in these brief sketches, the ugly and brutal face of war is glimpsed time and again among the routine and romance, the humour and hard times, and that special comradeship which flourished through interdependence.

I believe that these survivors have related their reminiscences with honesty, memories in many cases being reinforced by publications and documents of the day. Thus, I hope that contemporaries will read these accounts and think. "Yes, that was how it was." Also I wish that other generations of Canadians may learn and understand more about their compatriots, young people who were the flesh and blood associated with place names and cold statistics of 1939-1945.

Joyce Hibbert, Drummondville, 1985

SEA

WRENS personnel on the signal mast, HMCS *St. Hyacinthe,*
at St. Hyacinthe, Quebec in September, 1944.

1

Athenia Survivor

I'm not afraid of submarines or anything like that and I'll come back when I'm well."

Thirty-four-year-old **Barbara Bailey** was trying to reassure her parents as she bade them a tearful farewell in London, England. The date was 31 August 1939.

As HER PRIVATE world had been shattered in the preceding weeks, she knew she had to get away. Now she was off to Canada where she would help care for her brother's baby girl in Calgary.

By this move she would avoid a complete breakdown while trying to forget the man who had been the cause of her anguish: Reg, who had ended their fourteen-year-long 'understanding' when he had announced his engagement to a young girl. As though to purge him from her life Barbara wrote him that final letter.

> The Adelphi Hotel,
> Liverpool, England
> 1 September 1939

> ... And this Reg, is probably my last night in England – not for good – I am coming back when I am fit again. Tomorrow, who knows – we shall probably be at war but for the first time in many months I am calm, nothing is real.
> ... And now to forget – forget every second of happiness I had with you and to forget how many times and how deeply I have paid for it....

Because of her highly nervous state in the weeks before her departure, there had been frequent tears and turmoil at home. From the Adelphi Hotel on that first of September she also wrote a letter to her mother.

> ... Several hotels seem to be closed down so was almost compelled to come here. It's dearer than I wanted but overwhelming attention.
> ... I feel much better already and am now off to enquire about the *Athenia*. Someone behind me is saying "I haven't said goodbye to my mother or anything – I've never done that before." That's just how I feel, terribly casual about leaving now.
> I ought to have brought my gas mask with me, everyone has a brown square parcel I see.
> I'll write again before sailing if possible....

The 15,000 ton Donaldson Atlantic Line steamship had embarked passengers at Glasgow and Belfast. With this final group boarding at Liverpool her passengers and crew would total 1400 persons. The *Athenia* was bound for Montreal carrying British, Canadian, and American citizens, as well as about sixty European emigrants and refugees fleeing Nazi oppression.

Barbara Bailey's valuables went down with the ship's safe.

1026
DONALDSON ATLANTIC LINE

RECEIPT FOR VALUABLES

T.S.S. *Athenia*
At Sea *3/9/39* 19

Receive from M*rs* *B N Bailey*
(1) *one sealed Package said to contain Valuables for safe keeping.*

As no charge is made, the Company do not hold themselves responsible for any loss or damage which may occur.

Passengers must call for their Valuables the night before arrival.

_____ Purser.

As she boarded the already blacked-out liner, Barbara Bailey had the immediate and disquieting impression that the *Athenia* was over-crowded. (According to 4 September 1939 edition of the *The Evening News*, the *Athenia* had the largest number of passengers on board for many years.) She was annoyed at having to share a cabin with the three other women already in it. Some husbands and wives had been separated for the voyage in order to permit four women or four men to a cabin.

Late in the afternoon of Saturday, 2 September the ship sailed out of Liverpool.

Next morning, free of seasickness, Barbara Bailey attended shipboard church service and afterwards joined the sober-faced passengers clustered around a notice board. In shocked silence they were reading a bulletin announcing Britain's declaration of war against Germany.

As if sleepwalking, she continued on her way to the dining room where the atmosphere was heavy with gloom. Her personal control broke and she burst into tears. One of the stewards urged her to pull herself together and quietly encouraged her to begin her lunch. To help, he even fed her a few spoonfuls of soup. War, she was wondering, what would it mean? An exchange on deck that afternoon had topical significance. "We will bomb Croydon" a German woman boasted, to which Barbara started to retort "When we bomb Berlin ..." Whereupon the woman had interrupted "I don't think we've considered that." The Englishwoman had the last word. "If you can get to Croydon, we can get to Berlin!".

Thus the ship buzzed with talk of war and Barbara Bailey sensed that people were greatly relieved to be on their way to North America, and away from it all. Indeed, she felt that she might be the only passenger feeling guilty and distressed about leaving Britain behind at such a perilous time.

While the First Sitting group were at dinner that evening Barbara lined up for a previously reserved bath. But the Second Sitting gong sounded and she had to miss it. Hurriedly she put on her bright reddish-mauve dinner dress, brown leather shoes with slatted fronts, and grabbed the matching handbag. She sat at a table with four other women. The sixth place was reserved for the Chief Radio Officer. His seat would remain empty. She began eating her cold salmon....

Next day, 4 September, Mr. Winston Churchill, First Lord of the Admiralty, rose in the British House of Commons to make a statement. He began:

"I regret to inform the House that a signal was received at the Admiralty about 11 p.m. last night giving the information that S.S. *Athenia* had been torpedoed in a position about 200 miles north-west of Ireland at 8:59 p.m....."

The news of the swift and brutal attack on an unarmed passenger liner was to reverberate around the world. Three quarters of her passengers were women and children, 311 passengers were neutral Americans, and 112 lives were lost.

"I remember a tremendous shattering bang ... lights going out ... the ship lurching ... shouts ... excitement!" Barbara Bailey would relate.

It was at that precise time – the moment of explosion – that she felt her common sense and recent Civil Defence training taking over. "AVOID PANIC AT ALL COSTS", that was rule Number One.

As diners began to rush, pushing and screaming toward the main stairs, she urged the two women nearest her at the table to keep their heads. "Let's wait, we may be doomed but don't let's get crushed to death," she begged.

Through the din they could hear the loud authoritative voice of a ship's officer. "KEEP CALM", he kept repeating over and over again. He peered into the dimness of the large debris-strewn dining room.

"Is anyone still in here?". Barbara Bailey explained that they'd waited for the end of the rush.

"Leave now," he ordered. Obediently the three women made their way up the stairs through the remains of tables, chairs, crockery and potted plants which had been swept along and upwards by the frantic passengers.

Suddenly Barbara thought that she ought to be wearing her life-preserver and coat. She turned and went back below groping about in the darkness while unsuccessfully trying to locate her own cabin. Fighting the choking fumes in the passageways and stumbling over cabin trunks, she eventually found a lifejacket and warm coat. Then as quickly as possible she went back up on deck.

"Passengers were running about, calling out names of loved ones. Some people had been blown into the sea when the torpedo hit. I looked down into the water and saw a woman's body floating by, clothes ballooned out. My mind reluctantly registered 'dead'.

"I noticed that many passengers had no warm clothing and started out to go below to see whether I could find some blankets but my way was firmly barred by a determined stewardess. By this time I realized that I was perfectly self-possessed and acting as though it were an everyday event for me to be shipwrecked."

She recognized the kindly steward from the dining room. He was hunched over and shaking. Their roles reversed, she grasped his shoulders telling him to control himself and give some help where he could.

Snatches of talk reached her, "... yes, they'd been hit by a torpedo, ... one man had seen a submarine's conning tower."

Wandering about the ship, she saw that several lifeboats on one side of the *Athenia* were damaged. Ship's crew, with help from passengers, were manning stations; one lifeboat had already been successfully lowered into the water. Saying a silent prayer as she watched some passengers tipped out of another on its erratic downward journey, she could only hope that the poor devils would be picked up.

Still wandering, she began consciously searching for a less crowded lifeboat station. Up on the boat deck she was hailed by a man in charge of a station and he insisted that she get into Lifeboat 8A.

"I looked over the side of the listing *Athenia* and far below there was a bobbing lifeboat seemingly full of people. I decided to obey the man's order anyway. I laid my handbag down and asked one of the men to tear my skirt so that if necessary, I could jump more easily. He ripped the skirt up one side and helped me attach my handbag to my belt. Then wishing me luck and instructing me to hang on to the steel cable leading to the lifeboat, he sent me over the side. Down and down I went, hand over hand with feet sliding on and off the cable until finally they came to rest on a ledge. Someone pulled at the hawser sharply – I felt more movement – and imagined that the lifeboat below was moving away. Was this the end for me? Should I drop into the water and take my chances? Just then a voice yelled 'Come on, you're doing fine.' My ankles were gripped and I was literally thrown into the lifeboat on top of others. We pulled away immediately. We were seventy living and one dead."

In sole charge of 8A, a navy blue-jerseyed seaman gave instructions, kept order, and worked unceasingly. Barbara Bailey was to remember him by the name Eileen embroidered on his seaman's jersey but never learned his real name.

The passengers were packed like sardines and suffering the miseries of seasickness. They had no choice but to vomit on themselves and each other. Sea water washed around their ankles, and knees met those of the person opposite. A little girl near Barbara began to scream. Again the advice "AVOID PANIC" flashed through her mind and Barbara Bailey clapped a hand over the child's mouth.

Seaman Eileen was careful to steer his boat away from the bright silvery path cast by the moon.

The one undamaged motorboat from the *Athenia* approached. A male voice announced that two more passengers needed space in the lifeboat. Eileen objected, shouting that they were overcrowded already. "They're coming anyway" was the reply and before she had time to brace herself a man's body landed on Barbara Bailey's back. Then others placed their arms across her back to break the force of the second man's arrival. The men brought news that a radio message had been received on the *Athenia* that rescue was on the way. One of the newcomers had a bottle of whisky. Barbara Bailey asked for a drink but the whiskey was not for sharing.

In that long uncomfortable and frightening night, Lifeboat 8A was being rowed steadily further and further away from the *Athenia's* listing hulk. Help was indeed on the way; a Norwegian merchantman was steaming towards them.

"Its twinkling lights reminded me of a fairy castle. I'll never forget the sight of the *Knute Nelson* as she came full speed to our rescue."

Yet at first sighting Barbara Bailey had had misgivings about the vessel and speculated out loud that it might be the German liner *Bremen*. The idea alone was enough to terrify the refugees. The men downed oars and the Jewish women set up an eerie wailing. Still doubtful about the ship's nationality she suggested to one frightened man that in order to conceal his identity, he should throw his passport overboard, which he did.

Fears were replaced by relief as the freighter's crew quickly implemented rescue operations. Barbara Bailey watched as women and children were hoisted aloft in a bosun's chair while men climbed up a swinging rope ladder. By the time it was her turn, a gangway had been lowered and it ended six to eight feet above her head. She stepped carefully over the body of a dead woman and was unceremoniously thrown by three men up into the arms of a huge young Norwegian sailor standing on the gangway.

Her ordeal in the lifeboat had lasted seven hours. "I had to climb over the side of the *Knute Nelson* where I was met by another big sailor who immediately took a knife to my lifejacket. One slash and it was off.

"In a small galley, where cockroaches abounded, I was issued a drink of gin. I took it outside and gave it to a terribly burned, half-naked man. Working below decks, he'd been badly scalded and salt water had got into the wounds. The poor man was obviously close to death.

It was late and I was exhausted. I looked for somewhere to sleep. The captain's and officer's quarters were packed with survivors. I saw a Polish woman toss aside the captain's clothes and hang her husband's long overcoat in their place. Damned cheek, I thought. About an hour after our rescue I bedded down on deck with a life-preserver as my pillow. I was hungry, cold, and tired. But oh! the joy of being alive!

"Toward dawn I heard a sailor shouting 'Hot drink. Hot drink." I followed him to a larger galley where he gave me a mug of something that tasted like coffee mixed with beef extract. The crew of the *Knute Nelson* were so kind giving us their beds, food, clothing, and willing attention., Food for the day was one egg, one potato in its jacket, one piece of hard tack biscuit, and tea. For these rations a little Cockney steward from the *Athenia* lined us up and kept a sharp eye out for any-one trying to get extras. The Poles in those distinctive long overcoats (under which they'd tried to smuggle possessions into lifeboats) got particular attention."

Walking into a room full of injured, Barbara Bailey found the sight and smell overpowering. In addition to the wounded, there were several women who had started heavy periods.

An injured man called her over. She noticed that his hands were badly burned and lacerated. Asking her to take his wallet from his pocket and look after it for him, he explained that he was an embassy clerk and his papers must be destroyed if the enemy should appear. Steel hawsers had burned and torn his hand when he helped lower a lifeboat full of people. Neverthe-less, the courageous Scot had rowed in one of the lifeboats.

Daylight came and in the distance they could see the doomed *Athenia*. On 5 September the *Knute Nelson* and her gallant crew reached Galway, Ireland carrying 430 *Athenia* survivors. Red Cross workers hurried aboard and removed the injured. Barbara Bailey had sustained a leg burn when she slid down the steel cable into the lifeboat. She accompanied the embassy clerk to hospital.

"I watched as they went to work on those damaged hands of his and then all of us – doctors and nurses included – drank a generous slug of whisky."

Before crossing to Glasgow, the survivors stayed two nights in Galway. During the first night Barbara Bailey, not surprisingly, had "a nightmare or something" which really frightened the other two women in the room.

8 September 1939

My dear Barbara,

We all had a very anxious time. Lottie telephoned at 8 o'clock on Monday morning and enquired whether you were with us. When I told her that you had left Liverpool on Saturday she said "Good God, the boat has been torpedoed."

... On Tuesday when we heard of those that had reached Glasgow and that you were not with them we rather lost heart. However your telegram reassured us.

We should dearly like to have you home but we feel that you alone should decide as to this. Life will be very dreary here particularly when it is dark and the perpetual dread of an air raid. Air raid warning on Tuesday morning for about two hours. If you go to Canada we shall feel that you and Fred are safe.

... Should you go to Canada your mother and I hope that we shall be spared to see you as soon as the War, which must be a terrible one, is over.

With fondest love,
Your affectionate father
Fred W. Bailey

Barbara Bailey, fit and determined, returned to live at Bookham Common near London for the duration of the Second World War. She firewatched, drove an ambulance and did office work for her solicitor father. The family home in East Dulwich was bombed three times and her parents were forced to move to their weekend bungalow at Bookham Common. The bungalow sustained bomb damage on two occasions.

Bookham Common was used extensively by the military and bombed frequently. It was on the Common that she met the Canadian soldier who became her husband.

19

The late Laura Bacon and her son Keith posed on the deck of the *Southern Cross*, a New York bound ship that rescued them after the sinking of the *Athenia*. Laura Bacon, the aunt of Stanley Salt of Chapter Three, is wearing replacement clothes given her for her wet torn ones, while the package under her arm is all that remained of her luggage.

Six and a half years after the *Athenia* sinking she sailed for Canada again; this time the ship was the grand old Cunarder, the *Aquitania*. Peacetime luxury liner turned troopship, she was converted again, into a war bride transport. Barbara Bailey was one of many hundreds of war brides on board bound for Halifax and points beyond.

Meanwhile, the Germans denied responsibility for the *Athenia* sinking. They claimed that she had been sunk by three British destroyers.

In January 1946 at the Nuremberg trials, the truth was revealed. During the case against Admiral Raeder a statement by Admiral Doenitz was read. In it he admitted that the *Athenia* was torpedoed by U-30 and that every effort was made to cover the fact. Those efforts began early with steps taken by the U-30 commander, Captain Lemp.

The commander contended that he had mistakenly identified the *Athenia* as an armed merchant cruiser. When he realized his error, Captain Lemp, later killed in action, hid his error by omitting to make an entry in his log book and by swearing his crew to secrecy.

An affidavit from Adolph Schmidt, a surviving member of the U-30 crew, was produced as evidence. He told of how, later in September when he had been severely wounded and due to disembark, Captain Lemp had presented him with a document insisting that he sign it. The wording was

> I, the undersigned, swear that I shall shroud in secrecy all happenings of 3 September 1939, on board U-30, regardless of whether foe or friend, and that I shall erase from memory all happenings of this day.

Was she haunted by the *Athenia* experience?

"Not until it came time for the first lifeboat drill. The war was over but I was appalled that many women kept on chattering and did not listen to instructions. Some didn't even bother attending. I discussed it with a war bride who'd been a survivor of a ship sunk in the Mediterranean. We both knew the importance of those drills." And both women were happy to sail to Canada and peace for their new married lives.

> **Barbara Bailey Durant,** *Athenia* survivor, settled on a small farm in the Ottawa region and worked alongside her husband.

2

Aboard the *Algonquin*

His time in the Royal Canadian Navy, and more especially the year on HMCS *Algonquin*, Welsh-born **Mervyn Davies** would never forget or regret; the close-knit 250 man unit, the good quarters, the taking of the fight to the enemy to hasten the end of the war, and he had had the great luck to have been a sailor who was never seasick.

HIS FIRST TASTE of life at sea had been in job-scarce 1929 when he had spent six weeks at Gravesend Sea School before signing up as crew on the *British Diplomat,* one of the largest oil tankers of the day.

"We sailed to Persia (now Iran), took on the oil and .... Norway, Belgium, and England. I was young .... as, I've been to sea – now I'll try

.... with the Westmount Police and .... nd in 1930 Mervyn too, left his .... nada. He found work in the ship- .... firm and in 1933 he sent for and .... hometown fiancee.

.... call of the sea that caused him to .... dren and the comforts of home in

.... ny duty to get into the war. My wife .... a bit about life aboard ship and I'd .... CN for some time before I was .... November was to HMCS *Dawson,* a .... erican Navy in the Pacific.

"As Leading .... Assistant, I was one of a team responsible for the ship's supplies which included all provisions and navy stores. Based in Dutch Harbour, we were convoying GIs and Sea Bees out to Amchitka in the Aleutians. There was little action in the area and the routine work lasted ten months. The usual razzing took place between Canadians and Americans. Once, when we were alongside a troopship in Dutch Harbour, the Yanks were teasing 'C'mon fellas, it's time for you to get your afternoon tea.' One of our boys checked his watch with 'So it is' and went below. He re-appeared carrying mugs and a bottle of rum. We drank a tot each and watched them drool."

Next it was back to HMCS *Naden,* the Victoria Base until his request for a transfer to Halifax to be nearer his family came through.

"Canada's first Fleet Class destroyer was almost ready for commissioning in Scotland and I was one of a hand-picked experienced crew ready to man her. They shipped us first to Charleston, South Carolina where a British cruiser from the Mediterranean pulled in for repairs. HMS *Arethusa* had been badly bombed and a temporary plate covered a gaping hole in her superstructure, a hole so big that you could have driven a railway engine through it. We heard that she'd lost 140 sailors when it happened. After six weeks of repairs she sailed for Britain with us as passengers, stopping at Newport for gun trials and then at the Azores to refuel. Local people came out from the islands in small boats. 'Buy this, or this, or this', they cajoled. 'You won't be able to get it in Britain.' I recall buying half a dozen lemons and stashing them in my gas mask container. Fellows would come in and sniff about, swearing they could smell lemons. I never let on or they might have vanished.

"The destroyer was still not quite ready and I was able to go on leave to Neath. Between trains at Crewe, I was taken aback at the sight of a woman porter hauling a great load of luggage. I gave her a hand and pushed, inquiring where I might get a bite to eat. I had a cup of tea and a sandwich on the station: God only knows what was in the sandwich, satisfying but tasting like sawdust.

"Hungry again when I arrived home at mid-morning, I kept wondering when my mother was going to feed me but the three of us sat and talked and talked. Then someone knocked at the front door, mother answered and put something in the pantry. Someone came to the back door and she went again. Then she cooked me a good feed of bacon and eggs. She'd had to borrow the food from neighbours and would return it in kind from the next week's rations. Food rations were small for two persons and she was thrilled to get my ration book, and the lemons. On my next visit I made sure that I took extra food to help them out."

Her crew boarded the newly-commissioned HMCS *Algonquin* 17 February 1944 and sailed to Scapa Flow to join the 26th Flotilla of the Home Fleet. The destroyer was kept busy on patrols, Russian convoy escort duties, and special naval operations along the enemy-held Norwegian coast. Davies recalls making three of those perishing cold and dangerous convoy runs up to Polygarnyy and back. The merchantmen would sail on to unload at Murmansk; only two ships were lost from the three convoys.

"We preferred rough weather because it limited U boat activities. In August 1944, on the early part of a Murmansk run, the first Canadian escort carrier, HMCS *Nabob,* was torpedoed off the Norwegian coast. She was hit astern and twenty-one men were lost. Other escort vessels including *Algonquin,* took on as many of the crew as could be accommodated. A number remained aboard the badly-damaged carrier and managed to get her back to Scapa Flow.

"We had little to do with the Russians at Polygarnyy; we did our job and they did theirs. If you went ashore to their canteen you had to climb up a steep winding path with a long-coated sentry posted at each turn. Musicians provided plenty of cheerful music and they sang a lot in the canteen. The language barrier stopped most communication but occasionally you'd meet a well-travelled merchant seaman who spoke some English. I gave one such chap a few cigarettes and he insisted I take two knives he'd made. I still have them.

"Sometimes we'd carry raiding parties of Commandos to points on the Norwegian coast and then return them to Britain when their mission was completed.

"In the spring of '44 we took part in special manoeuvres and training and everyone was guessing that the big one wasn't far

Ratings aboard HMCS *Algonquin* piling shell cases and sponging out guns after bombardment of Petit en Fer, France, 8 June 1944.

off. In late May we joined other ships gathering at the Isle of Wight."

6 June: Operations Neptune and Overlord were under way. HMCS *Algonquin* was in the vanguard of the 5000 – armada that crossed the English Channel that day. Behind the leading ships, others carried the army assault forces including the 3rd Canadian Infantry Division scheduled to attack Fortress Europe from Juno Beach, the code word for a stretch of Normandy coastline from St. Aubin-sur-Mer to Graye-sur-Mer.

"My regular action stations were to supply shells from the magazine to the 4.7 inch aft gun, and to man a depth charge with settings received from the bridge, but for the most part at invasion time I was working in the Code Room. Prior to the landing and in pre-dawn darkness, we took our offshore positions and demolished strategic buildings across the promenade with our 4.7 inch guns.

"Later in the day we knocked out a battery of three 88 mm guns two miles inland. We were in radio contact with army specialists who'd trained with us in Scotland. They'd been dropped in earlier and our man informed us that thirteen of our fifteen salvos had been direct hits on the battery. Behind us, the cruiser *Arethusa* and the battleship *Nelson* and other large warships were pouring shells on their specific targets much further inland.

"As time wore on, bodies of men killed in the assault action were being washed out from shore. When possible we'd take them up, check the identification tags, and bury them at sea. Wounded were taken aboard and attended to by our ship's doctor and his staff.

"My younger brother was in the British Commandos and passed by the Algonquin as he went in on D Day. Knowing that I served on her, he hollered trying to get someone's attention but without success. Hardly surprising that day. He told me about it later on when we were home on leave and enjoying our first reunion in fourteen years.

"On 7 June, I went on deck and watched numerous concrete caissons up to 60 feet long go floating by. They would be sunk to form part of the huge Mulberry Harbour. Dozens of old merchant ships were brought in to be deliberately sunk at high tide to form a "Gooseberry" or shallow breakwater. They

Burial at sea from HMCS *Algonquin*, 8 June 1944.

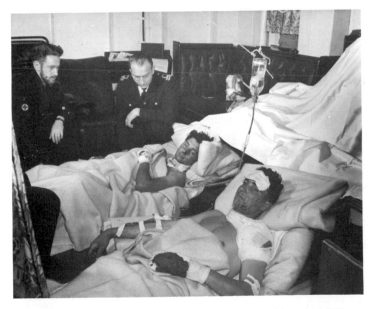

Two invasion survivors are cared for on HMCS *Algonquin*, June 1944.

A section of the shoreline at St. Aubin-sur-Mer, June 1944.

passed so close to us that one could see the face of each captain standing on his bridge – the faces reflecting the emotions of captains about to scuttle a ship. The Mulberry itself was an amazing sight when completed and all manner of supplies were unloaded from ships and rolled off on to the beach-head to fuel the Allied war machine."

Immediately following the initial invasion operations the *Algonquin* and sister destroyers patrolled up and down the embattled coastline, dealing with any remaining enemy strongpoints and on the lookout for pesky E. boats.

"The Germans had sown some new and effective acoustic mines that were attracted by the vibrations of ships' engines. We were about half a mile from HMS *Swift* when she caught one and went down fast but not before the secret radar equipment had been salvaged from her mast. Many of her crew were less fortunate.

"We carried Lieut-General H.D.G. Crerar, Commander of The First Canadian Army, and his staff over to France on D Day – 12. From informal chats with some of them, I gathered that they expected the war to be over within six months."

Shortly thereafter it was back to Scapa Flow and northern duties for HMCS *Algonquin*. One short and vicious operation code-named "Counterblast" took place on 12 November 1944. *Algonquin* was one of six warships attacking a German force carrying supplies to troops in Arctic Norway. Nine vessels, including ammunition ships in the convoy, were blown out of the water at the entrance to the Skagerrak.

At 2045 hours the Home Fleet ships were twelve miles from the coast and closing in. By 0102 hrs it was all over. In the middle of the fray the *Algonquin's* log recorded:

> 2325 Engage with all armament that will bear.
> 2330 *Algonquin* has hit two freighters and one escort, enemy on starboard beam 800 yards – one ship just blew up – tanker – shell passed between us and director – shore batteries opening up.
> 2335 Another ship blown up.

"It was horrible, horrible, to see those ships burning and know men were struggling for survival in the icy water. Under different conditions we'd have picked them up but no way could we risk losing our own ships and men by going in that close to shore. Their 8 inch shore guns were blasting away and when Admiral McGregor signalled from the cruiser HMS *Kent* to the effect – 'Come on boys, let's get the hell out of here ' – we were off.

"A real boost came on the way back to Scapa Flow when we received a personal message of congratulations and thanks from Winston Churchill."

In February 1945, a year and a lifetime after her commissioning, *Algonquin* was taking her original crew back to Canada.

"We ran into the worst storm of my experience. Some of her plates separated and water was rushing into the magazine. There was ice everywhere and when we came out of that, one of the crew developed appendicitis and instead of going straight to Halifax we had to put in at St. John's, Newfoundland."

Davies said goodbye to *Algonquin* in Halifax. It was home for leave, some marking of time in barracks, and then a job on the minesweeper, HMCS *Ungava*. After being sent aboard to straighten out the books, he stayed on that ship for several months.

Then VE Day arrived and with it, the Halifax riots.

"My impression was that nearly everyone was drunk that day. The navy felt that it had been treated shabbily in the war by some storekeepers who hiked up prices for the sailors. And then again, everything was shut up tight. They couldn't get home and there was nowhere for the thousands of young service people to buy a drink and celebrate the great occasion. They were frustrated to some extent but it was no excuse for the sort of behaviour that erupted. The mess and damage on Barrington Street was unbelievable. Disgusting. Unlimited drinking and the results. They'd broken into breweries and liquor stores, lugging out as much booze as they could carry. Members of the three services were there although the majority were navy. Some would pick up bottles, full or empty, swing them around and let them go smash through plate glass windows. It was a miracle that your shoes and feet were not cut to ribbons as you walked. Glass was everywhere. The servicemen did most of the damage but the civilians were quick to reap the benefits. They appeared with trucks to cart away the loot, even to three-piece chesterfield sets.

"The victory parade had just passed and my friend and I had seen enough. On our way back to the dockyard, we were passing the cemetery when a sailor stopped us and opened a club bag with 'Wanna buy a watch?'. The bag was half full of watches with price tags attached. We'd barely got a look when he closed it in our faces and took off. The Shore Patrol had just turned the corner.

"It wasn't long before the Shore Patrol arrived on our minesweeper; they were searching all vessels thoroughly and finding stuff hidden in air vents and other odd places. Those forewarned threw stolen articles overboard.

"After the chaotic day feelings were running high between the navy and civilian authorities. To help defuse matters the navy moved most of the ships out of Halifax Harbour. We sailed to Charlottetown for a few days."

Mervyn Davies left the RCNVR in November 1945 and returned to his textile job, later retiring to Picton, Ontario.

King George is piped aboard HMCS *Algonquin* at Scapa Flow, 1944.

3

Sinking of the *S.S. Sinkiang*

Radio Officer **Stanley Salt** was in the British Merchant Navy. In 1941, when only nineteen, the Derbyshireman encountered his wartime ordeal which he describes in this graphic account.

WHEN APRIL 1942, arrived the inhabitants of Calcutta were facing life with a sense of grim determination. Defence preparations were proceeding with the utmost expedition, the Japanese were pushing northward in Burma, and reports were circulating that the penal colony of the Andaman Islands had been occupied by the enemy.

"I was a Radio Operator at the time and assigned to ships operating in Indian coastal waters. I'd just returned from a short trip to Madras and during the trip it had become increasingly clear that the Bay of Bengal was no longer the peaceful, serene expanse of water that it had been at the beginning of the year. I began to envy fellow seafarers who were operating on the West cost of India; despite the heat of the Persian Gulf it was far healthier than the East coast where enemy subs lurked close to the beaches. And so, on 3 April it came as a welcome relief to me when I was assigned to the *S.S. Sinkiang*. From information I mustered after reporting for duty, I understood she was bound for Colombo and possibly the West Coast.

"She was a small ship even for coastal service. Tonnage 2646 and she carried a mixed crew. Her firemen and seamen were Chinese, the stewards Indian, and the officers British.

"We sailed the next morning, Easter Saturday. The *Sinkiang* nosed her way downstream through the muddy waters of the Hooghly shortly after dawn. Our first intimation of a troublesome voyage came after we'd been under way a little more than two hours. I picked up distress calls from ships anchored downstream between us and the estuary, in Diamond Harbour. They reported an aerial attack by a long range enemy seaplane. We arrived at Diamond Harbour late in the afternoon and anchored for the night. We could see little effect of the plane's visit, only one ship appeared slightly damaged.

"Aldis lamps began to blink at dawn the following morning as messages were exchanged. Shortly afterwards, one after another, sixteen anchors were hoisted from the mud and the ships fell into line ahead station, heading toward the open sea. Midday found us passing the pilot vessel stationed at the mouth of the Ganges. Emerging from the river, each ship took up its convoy station; four columns of four with the commodore ship, the *Tak Sang*, a fast China coaster, taking station number 31, i.e. third column from starboard, leading ship. We were joined by our only escort – two Blenheim bombers which flew in wide arcs to the eastward.

"Late that afternoon I was on watch listening to the incessant tropical static when loud distress signals suddenly came through the headphones. From their strength it was obvious the victim was not far away. She was the *Harpasa,* some forty miles astern and reporting that she was being bombed. One hit had disabled her steering and she was being abandoned. The *Sinkiang* was primarily designed for sailing around the China coast and was not fitted with voice-pipe communication from radio room to bridge. When I had a message on hand the only means of informing the bridge officer was to go outside and yell. Stepping outside to call for the quartermaster, I noticed the *Tak Sang* out in front of the convoy and altering course to retrace our own course. She was heading in the direction of the stricken *Harpasa.* We learned later that *Harpasa* should have been in the convoy but she had been delayed with engine trouble and was endeavouring to join us when the attack occurred. Sailing back through the columns, the commodore hoisted the signal 'All ships break convoy at sunset'. Those orders were executed. The ships scattered and slowly the gaps between them widened. We sailed on, southward through the night.

"Shortly before the first streaks of dawn appeared in the eastern sky, I commenced my watch. When our troubles began the sun was in full sight, the weather was perfect, and there was the slightest suggestion of a breeze over the deep swell of the calm sea.

"At approximately 6 a.m. distress calls started. This time from our companions of the previous day. One after another four ships reported being attacked by enemy aircraft. The attacks were uniform. It was zoom in, drop one bomb and then beat it. After the fourth there was a lull and I waited anxiously for the next transmission. The sudden noise of an aircraft skimming over our topmasts changed the direction of my attention. There was a splash, a flash, and a loud bang in the sea just off the port beam as a bomb exploded harmlessly in the water. I was soon transmitting our plea of distress and waiting tensely for the return run. All hands gathered at action stations and all eyes were glued to the skies but as the minutes ticked by no further attacks transpired. After a sufficient lapse, the old man gave the order for dispersal.

"By 8:30 a.m. the heat was pouring down and all hands were stripped to minimum apparel. Once again the silence of the ether was broken, this time by the most dreaded call of all merchantmen – 'Enemy surface raider'. A nearby ship reported sighting an enemy cruiser, then modified that to read 'two enemy cruisers and one aircraft-carrier'. Once again a ship in our immediate vicinity was the victim. In her next message she reported being shelled and at that point we could see the gun flashes in the distance. Only minutes later two ships took shape on the eastern horizon, a flat-top and a cruiser. The old man himself came running down from the bridge with a messeage for me to transmit. I began to tap out our plight to the listening shore station; RRR S.S. *Sinkiang* SIGHTED ENEMY CRUISER AND AIRCRAFT-CARRIER. The old man rushed back down again almost immediately. This time the news was worse. The message: BEING CHASED BY ENEMY CRUISER. I despatched it, then stole a glance through the porthole. The enemy ship was now assuming enormous proportions and coming up fast on the port quarter. Already I could see her for'ard gun turret trained on my radio room. Or so it seemed!

"On sighting the enemy we had changed our course and were now making a beeline for the nearest point of land which was about twenty-five miles away. In reality we never had a chance to make it against her superior speed. The next time I looked through the porthole there was no doubt in my mind that we were at point-blank range.

"Thoughts of my loved ones back home raced through my mind and I bade them a silent goodbye. I was waiting, waiting, waiting – expecting to be blown to pieces any moment. Then I did a peculiar thing. I walked to the door and closed it. That brought me a strange feeling of protection. I sat down again and then IT happened.

"I saw the flash of guns through the porthole, there was a terrific crash on board and the ship gave a heeling shudder. There was the alarming sound of escaping steam. My movements were almost automatic. The transmitter was still running and I started to send RRR *Sinkiang* BEING SHELLED ... halfway through there was another explosion as more shells struck. So far I was still intact so I carried on. Another flash and then a blinding one at starboard. With that my eardrums felt as though they were bursting and I was on the floor with the door beside me. The porthole wasn't there anymore. My radio room had been partially demolished.

"I soon discovered that I hadn't escaped scot free. I picked myself up and looked down at my feet which felt strangely warm and wet. Blood was pouring from gaping holes in my legs. Panic seized me. I tried to run and couldn't. Something was catching on my left ankle. A wood splinter, the size of an average piece of kindling, was protruding from just above my right ankle on the inside of my leg. I bent down, pulled, and it came out with a sucking sound. And then I ran. I jumped about four feet over a shell-hole in the deck and noticed the steam issuing from the engine-room skylight as I ran by. I was passing the old man's cabin when the next salvo struck. I don't know where it landed but the bang and shudder registered on my consciousness.

"I reached the starboard side where all hands still alive had gathered. Two Chinese seamen were trying to lower a boat under the direction of the old man. He took one look at my bloody legs and pointed to the boat. It was already three feet or so below the level of the boat deck and I had to jump down into it. I was looking around for the drain plug when the bow swung down, pitching me into the sea. As I landed in the drink the bow of the suspended lifeboat hit me in the back and dragged me under. I struggled free and floated astern, kicking out instinctively as the *Sinkiang* propeller passed me. The inertia of the ship was carrying her on.

"The distance between the two ships and myself widened rapidly and I became a spectator of the drama's final act. I watched salvo after salvo being pumped into the *Sinkiang*. At each hit, huge pieces of debris were flung some two hundred feet into the air, landing all around me, although by then I was a fair distance away. At last the end came. Her bow reared into the air and she went down almost perpendicular. A thick column of water spouted where she had been.

"The cruiser was under way immediately and soon disappeared from sight. I felt that my last human link had gone and I floated around feeling utterly lonely and convinced that I was the sole survivor. I knew that my kapok vest would keep me afloat for a reasonable time but there was always the possibility that my blood would attract sharks which abounded in those waters. I had no idea of time as I rode on the swell but I know it seemed like an eternity. Then I spotted an object about six hundred yards away and anxiously waited to rise again with the swell. Salvation was in sight! An empty lifeboat was wallowing around and I swam towards it. By that time my legs were feeling stiff, the right one was totally useless and I swam with it trailing. Slowly the distance decreased until at length I was alongside the boat. It was low in the water and by summoning all my diminishing strength, I dragged myself over.

"It was half full of water, I lay on the seat, weak through loss of blood. And lonely, terribly lonely.

"Much later (or so it seemed) I wondered whether my ears were deceiving me or was I hearing the sound of a swimmer approaching. There was a muffled grunt and two hands grasped the gunwale on the other side. Slowly the head appeared and then the body. My companion was Len the gunner, whose torn shorts revealed a nasty big wound in his right thigh. He lay down on the opposite seat, gritted his teeth and cursed our tormentors.

"'Bastards, bastards, dirty rotten bastards,' and then looking down into the water-logged boat 'Have to bale this leaky bastard out.' He groped around and came up with an empty can; I groped on my side and found the drinking water ladle. We began to bail.

"'Emptying yet another ladleful of water into the sea, I spotted a destroyer approaching. 'Better get down' I said to Len. We were aware of the Japanese reputation for machine-gunning survivors so we knelt in the bottom of the boat while peering cautiously over the gunwale. She came on until we could see the leering grins on the faces of her crew as they lined the rail. We crouched further down in the boat, fearful of the consequences should they spot us. After a few tense minutes Len could stand it no longer and stole a quick look. Relief showed in his eyes and voice, 'She's away,' he said. We observed her stern on, heading swiftly for the horizon. Then we went on bailing.

"That was when I looked at my watch and realized it was still going. The hands registered 10:30 a.m. My last message had been sent at 9:05 a.m.

"We were soon joined by more survivors. A few had miraculously escaped injury. Those from below were all suffering from scalds; the first salvo had been a direct hit in the boilers. When the Second Mate joined us he took command. The shrapnel holes in the boat were plugged with kapok from a torn life-jacket and the bailing continued until only a few inches of water remained. By 1 p.m. our numbers had swelled to twenty-one. The Mate had come aboard and he took over the command. The last ones to be picked up were the old man and the Second Engineer. The old man was clinging to a piece of wreckage with one hand and holding up the Second with the other. He'd been doing that for nearly four hours. The Second Engineer was in a pitiful state with his spine showing through the gaping hole in his back. He screamed in agony as he was hoisted over the gunwale.

"The lifeboat was now carrying maximum load and riding dangerously close to the water-line. The old man assumed command, ordered the oars manned, and we headed in the direction of the distant coastline.

"The sun beat down furiously and one of the gunners who'd been scalded over most of his body, began to lose his reason. The sun's heat aggravated his scald wounds to such an extent that his only wish was to leap into the cool sea and he had to be forcibly restrained. Each roll of the boat brought a hoarse cry of agony from the Second Engineer and he was pleading to be thrown overboard. Huddled in the bow lay the Chief Steward, another victim of the scalding steam. Around three o'clock he uttered a low weak moan and passed away, seemingly of shock. Lying in the bottom of the boat, immediately below me, was a Chinese seaman. The front of his shirt was an awful gory mess. Water washed back and forth over his face and no bubbles rose as it passed his mouth. He too, had died.

"Around four o'clock the breeze increased slightly so the oars were pulled and the sail hoisted. The oarsmen welcomed the rest and crawled around tending to the wounded.

"An almost paralyzing stiffness had set in over my whole body, the swinging lifeboat had injured my back, the wood splinter had punctured an artery, and I had open shrapnel wounds in both legs. To add to my discomfort the sun's heat created a terrible thirst. The freshwater keg was opened and the drinking ladle passed around. Although the water was brackish and oily it moistened our dry tongues and cracking lips. The cigarettes and matches were saturated; there was nothing to soothe our shattered nerves.

"It was slow progress but at last we entered a wide bay where black smoke was pouring from a grounded blazing Dutch freighter at the north end. In the centre of the bay a few native fishing boats rested on the beach in front of a small settlement of mud huts. There was a heavy surf running, another obstacle to overcome before we could reach the beach. The old man was dubious about attempting a landing but he decided that if we pulled down the sail and our oarsmen rowed with all their strength, it might be done. Native fisherman ran down to the beach to help us. As we came in with the surf, they seized the boat and dragged us to safety. No words were spoken as the natives carried the wounded to the sanctuary of that dry sandy beach.

"I lay on the warm sand and once again blood was spurting from the artery and my head began to swim. The village spokesman who seemed to be the headman went round with a black earthenware pitcher. He came over to me, placed the drinking hole to my lips and when the burning liquid had trickled down my throat, my dizziness was dispersed. The native brew helped boost our flagging spirits.

"One of our surviving Indian stewards acted as interpreter and we learned that we were seven miles from the nearest doctor — with no transport available. It was arranged that one of the local people would act as guide while two of our party would go with him to summon aid. After they'd gone we were moved to the shelter of a hollow in the sand dunes that headed the beach. At sunset we settled ourselves to await the return of our aid seekers.

"As we lay there in the dark a cool breeze sprang up and it soon became apparent that a storm was brewing. Lightning forked down on the sea while the rain increased in intensity until it became a torrential tropical downpour. The village huts were situated back from the beach to afford them shelter from the monsoons that occasionally swept the area. Shortly after the rain commenced the natives invited us to their huts.

Two men carried me and my back was filled with excruciating pain. One of the bearers placed his hand in the centre to support me; I yelled for him to remove it but he kept it there – and with his free hand helped himself to my wallet from the pocket of my shorts. This gave me considerable misgivings as to the motives of our apparent saviours but after we arrived in their dwellings and the womenfolk fed us from a communal dish of rice stew, my confidence returned. I had merely been the victim of an opportunist.

"In the early hours of the morning our first sign of aid appeared. The keen-eyed natives spotted a pinpoint of light. Its progress seemed outrageously slow and we waited for its reappearance each time the flashlight carrier had been obscured by vegetation. At last the solitary figure was silhouetted against the light of a hut and soon we were receiving our first medical attention. The Indian doctor did his best with his scant supplies. Counting the men who needed morphine, he found nine. He had only eight shots and Len the gunner volunteered to be the unlucky one.

"Before the morphine took its effect on me I heard the old man extracting the information we all awaited. The English-speaking doctor informed him that the nearest hospital able to provide adequate treatment for our men was ninety miles off in Vizagapatam. There was a small native hospital at Chicacole, fourteen miles away but no surgery was performed there and some of our wounded were in urgent need of surgery. It was seven miles to a mission at the nearest road point. The villagers possessed three ox-carts and were persuaded by the doctor to put them at our disposal; we were to make for the mission at dawn. I woke from my drug-induced sleep in daylight and to the sound of raised voices coming from the village compound. The natives were unwilling to harness their oxen without an extortionate fee for the services. The old man gave them a promise that this would be forthcoming and they reluctantly set to work preparing the carts. We were loaded into the straw-filled primitive conveyances and set off. Swaying from side to side, we bumped over the trackless baked earth, and each time we rolled over a bump we were thrown painfully against one another. The drivers cracked the slow-gaited beasts resoundingly on the rumps while urging the animals on, remaining completely oblivious to the sufferings of their passengers. The painful journey continued for over two hours until we reached the smoother surface of the road.

"The mission was a red metal building and we were welcomed by a Eurasian missionary who also supervised the unloading. We were placed very carefully upon thin straw mattresses on the floor of the little mission schoolroom and fed hot tea and sandwiches by our hosts. In the afternoon fresh transport arrived in the form of a delapidated old bus with open sides. And thus we continued our journey. The driver raced down the bumpy road at breakneck speed with the bus swaying sickenly at each bend. I was hanging on to the back of the seat with my good hand (my left one proved to be fractured) but eventually one turn was too much for me and I landed on the floor with an agonizing thud. This induced the driver to go a little slower and we arrived in Chicacole without further mishap.

"The tiny native hospital boasted a staff of one doctor and two nurses who worked on throughout the night as survivors from other ill-fated vessels continued to arrive. By next day about 200 seamen had been accommodated in the town, many of whom were wounded. The following day we learned that

Stanley Salt recuperated from his wounds for several months at the Presidency General Hospital, Calcutta.

Vizagapaptam had suffered an air raid and that the hospital staff there had been sadly depleted because some native members of the staff had absconded into the countryside. Now our nearest hospital was 200 miles away and too small to handle our numbers.

"Fortunately, the District Commissioner arrived the next day and he made the necessary arrangements for our removal to Calcutta. We arrived there on the Saturday, exactly five days after the *Sinkiang* had plunged to the ocean bed.

"Her Second Engineer was to die a few days later. My own injuries confined me to hospital in Calcutta for seven months and then to an additional five months of medical supervision which included repatriation and convalescence. I returned to sea duty in March 1944 and served until discharged in 1945."

Editor's Note: The Japanese Malaya Force under its Commander, Vice Admiral J. Ozawa, was responsible for the havoc created among Allied shipping in the Bay of Bengal in early April, 1942. The Malaya Force was deployed as part of 'C' Operation, Naval Operations in the Indian Ocean, March-April 1942 under C-in C Vice Admiral Nobutake Kondo.

A light aircraft carrier, five heavy cruisers, one light cruiser, and four destroyers constituted the Malaya Force. The force was split into three detachments on 5 April, and separated to attack specific targets on or close to the east coast of India.

Of the fifty-five merchant ships ordered to sea during the period 4-7 April, with S.S. *Sinkiang* among them, twenty were sunk with a total loss of 93,260 tons. Having virtually no protection and without naval escort vessels, the merchantmen were easy prey for the Japanese warships. All were attacked close inshore.

It was 1950 when **Stanley Salt** wrote this account of his five-day wartime ordeal. Obviously the sequence and details of the Bay of Bengal incident were vividly imprinted in his mind.

The Englishman had trained at Colwyn Bay Wireless College and joined his first ship in August, 1940. "Having always been fascinated by stories of foreign lands and peoples, I had a strong desire to travel."

In June 1941 he arrived in Montreal to join a large complement of seamen in the Montreal Pool. From this, Merchant

Navy crews were chosen to man the new 10,000 ton, 11 knot Liberty Ships as fast as they were completed in U.S. shipyards.

"I had a three month stay and during that time became completely enamoured of Canada, emigrating in 1948 with my charming Welsh wife and our small son."

For over twenty years **Stanley Salt** worked in the industrial electronics and parts distributorship field. Following that he was a property agent and appraiser but was forced to retire in 1980 due to ill health. His home is Lindsay, Ontario.

4

Salty Old Salt

Florence Tasker was an English girl working for the NAAFI (Navy, Army and Air Force Institute) at Oxshot, Surrey during WWII. She was to meet her husband-to-be, **Harold Tasker** in the canteen. He was serving with the 23rd Battery, 5th Medium Regiment, Royal Canadian Artillery.

Now FLORENCE'S FATHER was an ex-Royal Navy man and although a keen member of the Home Guard (the British local defence force) he'd never reconciled himself to wearing the khaki uniform.

The family lived near Blindley Heath and dad was in the habit of riding back and forth to work on his pedal bike. One evening he was somewhere between Nutfield and Goldstone on his way home in the blackout when he was hit by a Canadian Army truck. Three soldiers jumped out, assisted him into their truck, took him straight to a doctor and then to his home. They also saw to it that his bike was repaired and returned to him.

Although not seriously hurt, the older man was unable to work for a week or two because of painful bruising. The Canadians visited him at home several times and Florence remembers that her mother was touched by their genuine concern.

On one of their visits the young soldiers were suddenly convulsed with laughter and when it was over they apologized to their accident victim. The cause of their hilarity had been the recollection of his cussing at them when they'd helped him up. Apparently he'd given the army boys a never-to-be-forgotten sample of his old navy vocabulary – prolonged and without repetition!

Florence can still hear her mother's surprised and gently reproachful "Oh Alf, you didn't."

Harold and Florence Tasker live in Moose Jaw, Saskatchewan.

Uncle Joseph Watson
in his Home Guard
uniform.

5

To the Far Shore

The son of a deep sea captain, **Iver J. Gillen** was born in Victoria, British Columbia and moved to Vancouver at an early age. He joined the RCNVR (Royal Canadian Naval Voluntary Reserve) and when war was declared, he became a full-time sailor at the age of thirty.

CONCERNING THE period a week after D Day, the following excerpts are from papers containing his on-the-spot observations from 4 June 1944 until 7 September 1944. Based on his diary, this clear-cut account of events from a particular perspective, was donated to the Public Archives of Canada by the late **Iver J. Gillen,** ex-Leading Signalman V 14253.

"This is an account of the activities of one of Canada's corvettes in the English Channel during and after the invasion of the Continent. It is based on a diary kept by the writer; it contains no stories of big engagements, of heroic deeds; its mission, if it can claim one, is to show what life in the little ships was like. Those who served in similar ships – even some of my former shipmates – may disagree with me on certain points, but to the best of my knowledge I have kept to facts; I hope that which follows will prove of some interest to the reader whether he was there or not....

"To begin, the keeping of diaries or personal records of any sort is forbidden for obvious reasons in the Navy. A short time before the invasion began we were told that we might keep diaries if we wished, presumably to provide at a later date additional material for official records. If the latter were true, no advantage was taken of the chance to preserve our records for posterity, to my knowledge.

"My ship, HMCS *Camrose,* was one of the older corvettes, and had served in the Mediterranean during the North African campaign. Her type was laid down to carry a complement of about forty-five officers and men, and her armament consisted of a four inch naval gun forward and a light A/A gun aft. Revised, with the forecastle extended aft to the 'mid-ships superstructure, she carried between ninety-five and a hundred crew all told, and the armament was increased to 4 inch gun, pom-pom, and six 20 mm Oerlikons (A/A guns), – not to mention a great number of depth charges and certain other anti-submarine weapons. The Commanding Officer, Lieutenant Commander L.R. Pavillard, RCNVR ('The Mad Spaniard') had been with the ship since she had been commissioned, as had some of the crew. Prior to the opening of this record, *Camrose* had been one of a 'support group' on escort duty in the Bay of Biscay, running out of Londonderry. Late in April 1944 she was sent down to the Channel, and arrived in Portsmouth,

1 May. For about a month thereafter she was engaged in escort duty in the Channel, based in Portsmouth and Sheerness. Some of the escorted craft were ordinary merchantmen, but some were like nothing seen on earth before – parts of the pre-fabricated ports, and other odds and ends to do with the big event.

"My 'story' opens on 4 June 1944. We are at anchor in Weymouth Bay, off Portland; arrived here 28 June, and have had no contact with the shore at all. This is generally thought to be because we are about to take part in some large-scale operation; none of the officers seem to know what is in the wind, and we can think of no reason for keeping the ship so long in one place, after having been so busy the past four weeks. The harbour is quite a bustling place, crowded with American and British ships of many types, including the ubiquitous merchantmen. Landing ships and landing craft come and go hourly, and in fact everyone seems to be on the move except one group which remains quiet at anchor. It consists of *Camrose,* two other corvettes – *Lunenburg* and *Baddeck* – the old French battleship *Courbet,* and two tugs, *Samsonia* and *Growler. Courbet* is no longer a proud fighting ship; built in 1909, of 22,000 tons, she was scuttled in a port in Africa during France's dark days. She had been completely submerged, and the mark of the waterline was still visible on her towering foremast when we first saw her. No effort had been made to clean her up, and most of her big guns have been cut off at the turrets. Some new A/A guns have been mounted on her but this gives us no idea as to why she has been raised and brought here. We made several trips to her in our whaler, the first time on a legitimate search for fresh bread and vegetables – we have no yeast for baking, and get no supplies from shore. The first party to board her found her crew most hospitable, and possessed of a plentiful supply of rum and wine. They were an odd lot in a way; there were about a hundred Free French matelots, and a smaller number of British A/A gunners. Both made us welcome, being as glad as we were to have a change of any sort. A few of the huge mess decks had been cleaned up enough to provide temporary quarters, and the refreshments came up in all sorts of odd dishes and jugs from one of the huge dark caverns in this dead ship. None of the men aboard knows

48

where she is going but they are all 'travelling light', with a minimum of kit and equipment. We did get a little bread the first trip, and it became necessary to make similar calls on succeeding days – until the First Lieutenant noticed something odd about the boat's crew after one visit, and put an end to the business. Today, Sunday, was a special occasion in our ship – we had 'Divisions' for the first time since leaving our own country. 'Divisions' is a sort of ceremony designed to make a sailor truly grateful for the Sundays it is omitted. It means all hands turn to and clean up the ship or establishment, while every man heckles and harasses his junior. Then, when so ordered, you change into your number one uniform, and clean up the mess you have just made doing so. Then, while giving your uniform a final brush over, you try to think of a place to hide or a legitimate excuse for dodging 'Divisions'. The effort is usually in vain, so when the quartermaster pipes 'Hands Fall In' away you go with the rest and fall in with your own division (seamen, stokers, etc.). A corvette has no clear deck space large enough for this purpose, but we assembled in some sort of order on the forecastle head. After being inspected, we were addressed by the 'Old Man', who told us we will soon see some real action.... In the afternoon a privileged few, myself among them, were told enough to make it quite clear why we are waiting here. We have aboard secret orders for 'Operation Neptune', (Code name for naval part of 'Overlord') the invasion of the continent. Our part in the opening phase is relatively small, but of many such small parts a mighty machine has been built. We are to escort *Courbet* across the Channel to a place in the Seine Bay, the site of one of the two proposed artificial harbours – the 'Prefabricated Ports' which are the foundation of the plan. Our destination is known by the code name 'Mulberry B', and *Courbet* is to be sunk to form part of a breakwater there.... We now await the signal which will tell us to carry out our orders.

"5 June: Looks as if the big event is not far off; all day shipping in the bay has been passing the boom, outward, in a steady procession. By evening there is only our little group left, and without the *Lunenburg*, she having been sent out to another job. Just before supper we received the signal which told us in a few short words that the big job begins before

A line of blockships were sunk at high tide to form a shallow breakwater.

"Gooseberry", a line of blockships laid off the beach to form a reef before the rest of the Mulberry was assembled.

dawn.... At about 2340 we were privileged to witness part of what must have been the most dramatic and beautiful spectacle of the whole war – the first of the great air armada, the vanguard of invasion, leaving the shores of England for Normandy. Out of the dusk, over the hills they came, flying low – bombers, troop transports, gliders in tow, in groups of 35 to 50. Each plane was burning red and green sidelights, white light in tail, and bright white Morse light under the fuselage; the combined effect of these made each group look like a cluster of brilliant jewels floating through space. Hour after hour, through the night, they roared off into the darkness; and the sight of them – the thought that here was history being made, found most of us with little to say.

"6 June: 'D-Day'. Formations of our aircraft still passing over until about 0400 by which time a good many of them had returned empty to base.... At 0700 the BBC gave the world the news it had awaited so long – that the landings had been effected on the coast of France, near the Seine estuary, and the first phase of the invasion was a success.... We now are told that we do not sail until tomorrow, and I guess most of us feel a bit of a letdown at missing the first act. However, since we know little of what actually went on over there, we might count ourselves fortunate to be still safe in harbour. In the evening, about 1950, formations of planes towing gliders began passing over, bound for France, and kept on continuously for three and a half hours.

"7 June: At 0700 weighed anchor, and proceeded out of harbour, with *Baddeck* (we are Senior Officer), and two tugs towing *Courbet* one on each bow, speed about three knots. Planes towing gliders again overhead; continuous activity in air all day, planes going to, and returning from France. Day uneventful otherwise; weather fine, but not very warm.... Our ship's company had been put into two watches (known as defence watches) for dark hours and emergency of any kind. We closed up at our action stations tonight at dusk 2230. At the same time had to reduce speed, as we are ahead of schedule. About midnight some E-boat activity near, but not involving us. We have ships all around us, literally, and one just astern of us got an E-boat in the beam of her searchlight. When she opened fire we could see the fall of shot with the naked eye. Then after a moment of darkness something – presumably the E-boat – burst into flames which were visible to us for nearly an hour. There followed almost continuous explosions from the burning vessel, and we could see a ship standing by her.... On this and subsequent nights there was so little W/T and R/T traffic that we could never tell what went on around us, even within visual range.

"8 June: Shortly after midnight we began hearing the big guns near the beaches, the Old Man estimates our position as about 14 miles off the coast, and some of the reports or explosions made our little ship shake. About 0100 an enemy air attack on the beach ahead of us began, and they were soon dispersed by a very heavy A/A barrage. We saw one plane brought down in flames.... Considerable activity at sea in our vicinity during the dark hours preceding dawn – bursts of Oerlikon tracer and many star shells. At daybreak we were quite close to the shore, but it was hidden by mist. At 0800 the mist was gone, and we got our first look at the coast of France – what was visible through and over the ships of the great invasion fleet. Very little confusion; a great movement of small craft, but all the big ships – the men-of-war, hospital ships, supply ships, etc., seem to have found their places in the pattern and settled down to await orders from NCXF (Naval Commander Expeditionary Force). We cruised up and down the beach area in search of this or some other senior officer: *Courbet* having gone to her 'berth', our job is finished, and we do not know what we are to do next.

... Within the limits of the beach area we can see what appear to be three towns; our officers think the larger one is Ouistreham, and neither it nor the others appear much damaged. We can see tanks, trucks, and other vehicles moving up the slight incline from the beach as they leave the landing craft. Weather fair, but a moderate wind and sea is hindering landing of men and equipment a little. Some of our heavier ships – *Rodney, Nelson,* and some cruisers, are shelling the country back of the beach-head.... About 1330 a great column of smoke arose from one of the towns.... There are few signs from seaward of German resistance to the landings, except for several wrecked landing craft on the beach. Some distance off shore, but in shallow water, is the wreck of the R.N. 'Captain' class frigate *Lawford*. Sunk while at anchor yesterday, she broke in half amidships; the broken midships section now rests on the bottom, with the bow and stern above water. We learned later that there was little loss of life – and also that the cause of the damage was not known; just a heavy explosion that could have been mine, torpedo, or bomb.... We finally anchored near one of the Control ships which direct traffic; got orders from her to sail with *Baddeck* for Portsmouth; under way at 1515. Weather is deteriorating. Passed many landing craft and tugs with tows of various types bound for far shore. (This latter was the term for the French coast used in all official communications, and soon came into common usage.) At 2215 we passed the Nab Tower, receiving orders from the signal station there to anchor at Cowes. Anchorage full of merchantmen ready to sail.

"9 June: Weighed anchor at 0900, proceeded to Fleet Oiler *Teakwood* to top up with fuel oil. Returned to anchorage at Cowes about 1500, on two hours notice for steam – which means that the ship must be in all respects ready to put to sea within two hours after being ordered to do so.

"10 June: Saturday. Usual routine carried out – everything above and below decks cleaned and squared up in morning, 'Make-and-Mend' in afternoon. The new 'revised' type corvette *Louisburg* is anchored near us, and we were able to exchange visits with some of her crew. Very nice ship, not much like the older ones."

Incidentally, *Louisburg* replaces the first corvette of that name, sunk in the Mediterranean in a torpedo-bomber attack on a convoy; *Camrose* was in the same group, as was *Kitchener*, the ship on which **Iver Gillen** was serving then.

"11 June: Prospect of a quiet Sunday spoiled by receipt of a signal in late afternoon ordering us to proceed out of harbour. Under way with *Baddeck* by 1140. We are to patrol Channel 56, one of the routes to the far shore, and escort part of the way any tugs with tows, or convoys, that come along. Weather fair – cloudy, with occasional rain. At dusk we picked up two pairs of tugs with 'Whale' tows (parts of the prefabricated ports) and stayed with them during the night. All during dark hours displays of starshell and tracer shells visible.

"12 June: About 0430 saw and heard numerous heavy

explosions in direction of French coast and some A/A fire in same place; looks like many another air attack. Left our tugs and tows at daybreak. At 0730 came upon two more tugs with a Whale tow, having some difficulty with same. As near as I can describe them, 'Whales' were heavy sections of floating roads or ramps, buoyed up by big steel tanks; there were usually four or five sections in a tow, and in this case, the after two tanks had leaked and sunk. The towboat skippers said further towing was impossible, as one tank was already on the bottom. They could not just cut it loose and leave it as it was a menance to navigation, and they had no alternative but to stand by until someone came to assist them. Our Old Man decided to sink the lot by gunfire, after salvaging what could be removed. Sent a small boat away, but it was found that of all the valuable gear stowed on top of the whales (small landing craft, coils of wire cable, miscellaneous Army equipment) most was too heavy to move. The tug captains assured our CO that the bouyant tanks were filled with petrol, so we stood well off before opening fire. The first hit released only air, so we closed in and used all our guns. It took nearly three hours to sink the thing – which could be a tribute to the builders or a reflection on our gunners. Hardly the latter, as many direct hits were scored with little effect. Difficult target to hit, low in the water, rising and falling in the slight sea, and many shots just glanced off the tanks.... During this bit of war effort two R.N. destroyers passed us at high speed, bound for far shore. They asked us by light what we were doing, and on being told, asked us to hold our fire until they were past. (Later found out that one had aboard Winston Churchill, on his way to visit the beach area.) Today forenoon we passed five bodies floating on the surface – two airmen and three seamen. One of the former was sitting bolt upright as if in a chair, held so by his lifejacket, head and shoulders out of the water. An occasional wave now and then washed over him, smoothing back his hair as if with a comb. This gruesome sight seemed to fascinate some of the newer members of the crew, to whom a casualty was something one read about in the papers. It brought home to them rather abruptly the fact that war is more than bands and uniforms, seeing the world and being a hero in the home town. For a few it also emphasized the fact – more than our officers had been able to do – that it might be smart to stay wide awake on watch. Easy now too, to enforce the standing orders regarding wearing or carrying of life-jackets. Some criticism of the Old Man for not stopping to recover, attempt to identify, and properly bury the dead, as we know one other Canadian CO has done. However, our Skipper is wise; aside from the fact that the Germans have been known to attach mines to floating bodies, submarines are becoming active in the Channel, and a ship hove to would be an easy target. Passed much fresh wreckage, and two lifeboats which we took alongside and stripped of equipment. Weather better and getting warmer. In forenoon met tug *Growler* with Mulberry tow, and escorted her to end of Channel 56. About 1600 we were ordered by signal to return to Portsmouth. Had been about two hours on way when we received another W/T signal to meet and escort two more tugs with Mulberry tows for far shore, speed four knots. Met them about 1830, and were joined by *Baddeck* and *Louisburg*. Just after dark starshell began to go up all around us, some much too close for comfort since it illuminated us. We learn by signal that there are about eight E-boats in our vicinity. About 2230 there was a tremendous barrage of A/A fire along the French coast, and we saw many bombs exploding, lighting up the sky; the detonations can be felt aboard us, though we are about 15 miles off shore. The attack kept up all night, and the noise was added to by gunfire from our big ships at the beach area – they have some target not very far inland. Some very colourful tracer shell displays in our vicinity, but as usual we do not know who is firing.

"13 June: A few minutes after midnight *Louisburg*, on our starboard quarter, got a radar contact; she reported it to us, and illuminated with starshell. The latter were laid accurately over two E-boats making for our little convoy. Owing to their speed and evasive action she soon lost them, but we picked them up a few seconds later by radar and also illuminated them with starshell, some distance from the first position. Got away a few rounds of 4 inch and a lot of Oerlikon, and appeared to score more hits with latter, the range being close at times. Lost target when starshell burned out, and tried again with illuminating rockets; found target again, and opened fire, but this time they were going all out, half hidden in spray from their bows, and they were soon out of range and sight. The enemy hereabouts seems disinclined to take risks, and our two did not even return our fire. They might have done us some damage, as they have much greater speed and are armed with 40 mm guns. We investigated several radar and asdic contacts later, but nothing developed. Just before dawn a ship in another convoy near us was sunk, but we did not learn how, nor who she was. Made very poor time all day as the tow is very hard to handle. Nothing of interest during daylight; dark hours same as before...."

Editor's Note: The Royal Canadian Navy grew from thirteen vessels and 3,600 personnel at the outbreak of war to a force of 93,000 personnel and 939 vessels (373 categorized fighting ships). The RCN contributed 110 ships and 10,000 men to the Normandy landing operation.

Naval vessels built in Canada in the war period; 487 escort ships and minesweepers, 391 cargo vessels, 254 tugs and auxiliary vessels, 3,300 special purpose craft.

> At the war's end **Iver Gillen** transferred to the Merchant Service and eventually joined the Canadian Customs and Immigration Department. Upon his retirement in 1972, he and his wife Anne, went to live on Salt Spring Island, British Columbia where he died suddenly in October 1981.

Iver J. Gillen is on the far right of his four shipmates from across Canada.

LAND

On 5-7 November 1943. Black Watch on Assault Training.

6

Acceptance

Outside Greyshott, England, in September 1941, Canadian Army Chaplain **Waldo Smith** studied his map before his rounds. Recently in 1980 Waldo Smith had this comment on one consequence of the Second World War.

"My personal jeep had been 'modified' to serve as an ambulance if necessary. The ordnance section built a projection in the rear to support angle irons which would be the tracks to take stretchers. I had a canvas cover with a large red cross painted on each side. When the enemy saw this symbol they did not shoot at me.

FOR A GIRL TO marry a serviceman from overseas was a high risk gamble. She was too willing to believe the best of men who set themselves out to please. And in war's hazards the uniform did something to women. Many a man looked smart only because the provost sergeant had not let him out otherwise."

Close to 50,000 young women, the majority from Britain and Holland, took that gamble and married Canadian servicemen. For most of them, it was a happy choice.

Reverend W.E.L. Smith relayed the following poignant story connected with one such venture.

"A farm, a few miles north of Cobourg, Ontario was the destination of an English war bride and her infant son. Her husband, a farmer's son had arrived home ahead of her and was working with his father.

"Unfortunately, the mother bitterly resented the marriage and received the daughter-in-law unkindly. The poor girl had an unhappy time that winter. In spring she went into hospital for the birth of a second child.

"Grandmother was left in charge of the little boy, by then a toddler. One day she suddenly noticed that he was no longer with her. She hurried outside to look for and call him, but could find no trace. During the lapse of supervision he had found his way to a pond and drowned.

"The young war bride was told of the tragedy and prepared herself for the return to her husband's home. Carrying the newborn child she went into the farmhouse and greeted her mother-in-law with a warm smile. The older woman broke down, all bitterness gone."

Honourary Major **Waldo E. L. Smith** M.C. served overseas 1941-45 as chaplain with the 1st Canadian Armoured Brigade, the Canadian Army Service Corps and later with infantry as they attacked the Gothic Line. His book, *What Time The Tempest,* an account of his wartime experiences, was published by Ryerson Press in 1952. Rev W.E.L. Smith is a retired minister of the United Church living in Kingston, Ontario.

7

Here and There with a Hasty Pee

The Hastings and Prince Edward Regiment, an infantry unit of Canada's First Division was assembled primarily from men who joined up from the farming area, backwoods, and small towns of the two Ontario counties. Among them was **Robert Bate** of Bowanville, an employee of the Goodyear Tire and Rubber Company who served six years with the Hasty Pees.

Eʟʟʏ ɪɴ ᴛʜᴇ ᴡᴀʀ, leaves and humorous incidents punctuated the routine and discomfort. But then Sergeant R. Bate was catapulted into the hard-fought Italian campaign and faced the red-hot reality of front-line fighting. In common with so many combat soldiers, the ability to appreciate the lighter side of a deadly serious job never deserted him.

Shortly after enlistment he heard the story about two Hasty Pee men of 1939 who had climbed to the roof of a Picton canning factory-turned barracks to take down an imposing pewter figure of an Indian Chief. Thought to be a likeness of Tecumseh, the firm's trademark weighed in at 500 pounds and stood over eight feet tall. Adopted immediately as regimental mascot, Little Chief was within forty-eight hours on his way to Halifax with the overseas bound detachment. When the men fastened him to the prow of the troopship *Ormonde*, Little Chief was an impressive figure-head with his spear in one hand and his tomahawk in the other. From England the Hasty Pees and their mascot sailed to Brest in June 1940. After travelling 200 miles inland by train they were forced to return to the French coast. Little Chief had gone along with the transport section who at that point were ordered to damage, destroy and abandon vehicles and equipment. What should they do with the mascot? Because of his size and weight they wrapped him in groundsheets and buried him – with the intention of retrieving him later. Although several efforts were made to locate Little Chief after the war, he remains Missing in Action.

"Little Chief", mascot of the Hastings and Prince Edward Regiment in England, March 1943.

Back in Canada the Second Battalion commissioned Abe Patterson of Pembroke to carve a proud new 500 pound mascot. Named Chief Petawawa-Much, he was assigned the number C.0001 and shipped overseas to the First Battalion in England.

Meanwhile in Picton, Bob Bate and a couple of friends had made plans to provide the new Chief with a mate.

"We'd noticed a statue of an Indian maiden standing on a pile of rocks outside a summer resort place on the road between Belleville and Trenton. We figured that she could go overseas with the next draft. Ours. One night three of us drove over there in my car, cut her down with pliers, took her back to Picton and left her in the Officers Mess. When we moved to Camp Borden she was crated up and went on the train with us. But by then some newspaperman had got hold of the story and her photo appeared in the Picton paper. Her owner demanded six hundred dollars or her return. We'd have had trouble scraping together six hundred cents right then so our plan fizzled and she was taken back to her pile of rocks."

Ex-Sergeant Bate still chuckles at the memory of a startling trick once played on a sergeant-major 'who was always after us'. The object – 'to shake him up a bit!'. In Possingworth Park, Sussex, the sergeant-major's quarters were in a quonset hut. One night the troublemakers began their lark by first fixing props against the outside of his hut door, a bag was put over the chimney and smoke quickly filled the hut. When a window was thrown up, they immediately threw a thunder-flash in and there was a loud explosion. Thunderflashes were harmless but the explosion resembled the sound of a dangerous hand-grenade going off. The well-executed prank was a shaker alright, and the penalty came the next day when the battalion was ordered out on a forced march. Not a favourite pastime, even for infantrymen.

A youthful Farley Mowat would join the Hasty Pees in Italy. Bob Bate was Orderly Sergeant of the Day to Farley Mowat's Orderly Officer of the Day when they met for the first time.

"I went to the door of the Officers Mess and asked for Lieutenant Mowat. When he appeared, I thought to myself, God! What are they sending us now – Schoolboys?".

Four dispatch riders of the Hastings and Prince Edward Regiment in England.

Later, they had been fighting in the battle for Ortona and were withdrawn for what was termed a rest.

"Every forty-eight hours our trucks would go back down to Company HQ for rations. This particular night they'd arrived back and the lead truck had parked outside my tent. Early in the morning I woke to a strange scratching noise. I found it was coming from the back of that truck. And what was scuffling about in there but a live turkey! I hollered up the driver, 'Where the devil'd you get that bird?. ' He gave me some story about finding it on his way back to camp. 'Well, you'd better do something about it before they come round on inspection' I told him. So he set about killing it, burying feathers, etc. and then cut it up. We found a cooking pot and looked forward to a good feed.

"About 10 a.m. I was sitting there by the fire we'd made when the Orderly Officer, Lieutenant Mowat, and the sergeant came by.

" 'What's in the pot, sergeant?'

" 'Beef sir. It came up with the rations last night.'

"It seemed to satisfy them but they were still looking around as they walked away. Then Lt. Mowat spoke again.

'Let me know if you hear of anyone finding a turkey. The officers were supposed to have one for dinner today and it disappeared in the night.'

"So there I was. Sitting right next to the pot containing the bird in question. Wings, legs, and all. And lying about it, too. I was glad when that damned turkey was eaten."

Sergeant Bate entered a barn in Italy where several Hasty Pees were sheltering. One, Ted Sheehan, was wounded and had been placed in a manger. Bate walked over and quipped "Playing Jesus, eh" and remembers how it caused the man to smile through his pain.

His active soldiering came to an end when be became a casualty of war in Italy on 4 December 1943. The regiment was moving up toward the Lamone River and Bob Bate is convinced that he had two distinct but inexplicable warnings of danger.

"From the first I had a definite uneasiness about the move. I just didn't like the feel of it. But orders were orders.

"There were no bridges left across the river so we were to cross in canvas boats carrying piat guns and mines with us. The PIATs (Projector Infantry Anti-Tanks) would be set in position and beyond them, the mines would blow as track vehicles came on, and then the PIATs would get a crack at them.

"But the enemy caught on and we found ourselves in the middle of an artillery barrage. My runner and I lay facing the canal. Suddenly something told me – quite clearly – 'Turn around and get your feet towards the water'. I turned. And told Termite Kehoe to do the same. We protected our heads the best we could with our steel helmets. Then there was this blinding flash and we were hit.

"Now your army manual emphasized that you should never turn your back on the enemy but if I hadn't turned around I'd have got it through the neck. Likely my head would have been severed. What was the voice? Call it God, instinct, sixth sense, whatever you like. I definitely heard it. And because I obeyed it, I stayed alive."

Robert Bate's right leg, between knee and ankle, had been shattered by shrapnel.

Back in Canada, he would spend from 18 April 1945 until 27 June 1946 undergoing seven operations and numerous grafts at the old hospital on Christie Street in Toronto. He expressed gratitude and admiration for the nursing and medical staff at the time. The long period of treatment and convalescence was made more bearable for him by the fun happenings, often instigated by the servicemen themselves. Bate believes that the staff also benefitted from the larks and good-natured ribbing because the doctors and nurses were under considerable strain caring for young men suffering from horrible war wounds.

"On 22 December 1945 Farley Mowat and his father came to the hospital. We talked for a while and suddenly Farley said, in that way of his, 'Want a firecracker?' Now, I'd known about a few things he'd got up to in the past and I was curious about any firecracker he was offering. Sure, I wanted one. So he produced something that looked exactly like a big firecracker, complete with wick. At the time I was forced to stay in a strange position with one hand fixed to my lower leg for the grafting. Farley put the firecracker under the bedclothes and they left. I managed to work the outer wrapping off with my feet. That firecracker was firewater. A bottle of Haig and Haig.

"Pat Gahagan from Peterborough, another Hasty Pee with leg wounds, was in the next bed. We were both disappointed at not going home for Christmas but on the 25th we enjoyed our Christmas dinner and then passed the Haig and Haig back and forth. In the afternoon along came Dr. Warren who wanted to put us through what were known as 'hot and cold, sharp and dull' tests. By that time we were getting more ornery about not going home, and refused to be poked and prodded on Christmas Day. We told Dr. Warren to stop bugging us or we'd let him have it. Well, on Boxing Day we were both loaded up and taken down to the Main Office and charged with Misbehaviour – specifically Drinking. And we were each fined five dollars!

"Once we fixed up a streetcar around one bedridden patient. This man had a cage over his injured legs. A fellow named Rutherford found two spotlights and fitted them on the front of the bed for headlights. We used a urinal bottle for a muffler and a rubber ring for the steering wheel. A couple of folding chairs were put alongside for passengers and then screens around. We put pictures on top of the screens like on a streetcar or bus. We found a bell and fixed up traffic lights. The 'driver' would turn up his radio full blast for engine noise and then take his pretend streetcar on its imaginary route. The nurses wondered what we'd be up to next.

Saskatchewan Drive, Ortona, Italy in February 1944.

"Two of the popular nursing sisters were named Barnes and Currie. One day Biddie Barnes was getting a fellow ready to go home. His speech had been badly affected and his hands damaged. We'd tease him a lot trying to get him to talk so as to help him. Anyway I suggested to Nurse Barnes 'Go on, give him a kiss, send him home right.'

" 'I will not'.

" 'Ah, but you would if he had a couple of pips. eh....' Well, she chased me around the ward. I was hobbling about by that time and when I jumped into bed, she dumped a jug of water and ice cubes over me and the bed.

"At 3 p.m. Barnes and Currie came into the ward in their capes ready to go off duty. By then the orderly had changed my mattress. 'Are you feeling better now?' Barnes asked me. Then before I could answer, she'd jumped my buddy Pat Gahagan who'd been mouthing off earlier, too. She pinched his nose while Currie reached over and poured castor oil in his mouth. Then she handed him a toilet roll with 'You'll be needing this before morning!' "

Robert Bate, now retired, still lives in Bowmanville, Ontario.

8

Lost Dentures and Un Peu de Bren

Lieutenant **Vladimir Ignatieff**, Calgary High-landers, standing outside the house used as A. Coy Headquarters at Eastbourne, England, 25 December 1941. Born in Kiev, the second of five sons in the family, Vladimir Paulovitch Ignatieff was thirteen when he left Russia.

Hᴉs ꜰᴀᴛʜᴇʀ, ᴄᴏᴜɴᴛ Paul Nicolaevitch Ignatieff, a governor of Kiev province, had been a popular and democratically-minded Minister of Education in the Czarist government. Although released after a short imprisonment by the Bolsheviks, Count Ignatieff nevertheless deemed it wise to leave the country. In July 1919, the family boarded a British transport at the Black Sea port of Novorossiysk. From Constantinople they made their way to France and thence to England where Count Ignatieff purchased a 200 acre farm near Hastings.

After attending St. Paul's School, young Vladimir studied at London University's Agriculture College at Wye. His older brother, an electrical engineer, who had emigrated to Canada was sending back glowing reports about the country and its opportunities. As one of a group of forty Wye students, Vladimir would spend most of his 1926 summer gaining practical harvesting experience in the Canadian West.

"We were sponsored but certainly not coddled by the CPR. We crossed the Atlantic in steerage. One fellow had packed his tuxedo and nightly crashed the First Class dances – until on the final night there was a hell of a row and he was exposed. He'd fancied the same girl as a jealous Purser who blew the whistle. We disembarked at Quebec and rode the comfortless colonist cars to Winnipeg. There the IODE ladies arranged for our farms and we were put to work, stooking for four dollars and thrashing for five dollars a day."

At Vladimir's urging the farm in England was sold in 1927 and his parents moved first to Montreal, then Toronto, and in 1936 they settled in Upper Melbourne, Quebec. By 1939 Vladimir had earned a Master's Degree in Soil Science from the University of Alberta and a Doctorate in Bio-Chemistry from the University of Toronto; he had married and fathered two children and he had looked for a position in Canada and Britain. It happened that while searching for work in England in 1936, he had met 'Mike' Pearson who was then Second Secretary in the office of the Canadian High Commissioner. When the University of Alberta offered him a lecturing post in their Department of Soil Science he did not hesitate to accept.

"Just prior to the war, the Department of Defence sent out questionnaires to professional and technical people informing them that, in case of hostilities, their services would be needed.

I filled out my form and when Canada declared war I wrote them saying, 'I'm ready, now what?' I was thanked and politely told that the best thing I could do was to stay where I was. I joined the university Canadian Officer Training Corps COTC as a private and went to camp in 1940. Then, being somewhat officious and never reluctant to take command, I took the exams that qualified me for a commission. My pay and allowances as a private would have totalled only ninety-five dollars a month, that was another factor. I received rapid clearance from the RCMP allowing me to hold a commission in any branch of the Canadian services. An investigation was normal procedure when the applicant was foreign born.

"On the day that France capitulated I remember thinking, My God, now the Brits are the only ones left! And that was the day I joined the Calgary Highlanders."

Florence Ignatieff took the children and returned to Toronto where her family lived. From 1941 until the war's end she worked as head dietician in a war supplies plant in Scarborough. During the most intensive production period at the fuse-filling plant, shifts worked around the clock seven days a week and Mrs. Ignatieff was responsible for 8000 meals every twenty-four hours.

In September 1941 Lieutenant Ignatieff was sent overseas. "The training was rigorous. Being thirty-six, I needed my rest, and I wasn't looking for the excitment and wild times likely to interest a younger man. In addition, I felt very much at home in Britain. Near Hastings, on a scheme in 1941, I found myself eating a haversack lunch in the grounds of a small church, surrounded by farmland belonging to our previous home.

"The long hours and fatigue were lightened by amusing incidents. We were set for a night exercise in the Eastbourne-Bexhill area and orders arrived to start off. 'Get the company on the move. Send out the runners' I shouted at Sergeant-Major Jones. But he delayed over by the cookhouse truck where he and the cook were searching for something in the grass. They explained that the cook had lost his upper plate. And not your ordinary free army teeth, they emphasized. Then why the devil hadn't he kept them in his mouth, I wondered. 'Sorry cookie, to hell with your bloody teeth!' I exploded. And off we went.

"Towards dawn we halted somewhere on the Downs and the cookhouse truck arrived. Following the unwritten rule that in the field it's the privates who eat first, the NCOs (non-commissioned officers) next and the officers last, the men lined up for the usual bacon and porridge. I brought up the rear and as cook stirred the remainder of the porridge he suddenly let out a whoop of joy. He'd found the false teeth! 'Cookie, God bless you' I said 'but I'll pass on the porridge today.'

"On another exercise I was acting 2 i/c, (Second in Command). It was one of those cold rainy English days and orders were NO FIRES lest they give positions away. Thoroughly chilled and miserable, I was resting at the foot of a tree when I noticed smoke rising from a nearby copse. Investigating, I came on a section gathered round a fire they'd built in a natural shallow depression. I can still see the woebegone look on the young corporal's face as I bore down on them bellowing 'Put out that blankety-blank fire!'. A big Irish lad, Private Donald O'Connell looked up casually with a bold 'Who says so?'. Now I'd done a lot of boxing and knew I could handle the situation so I propelled all 6 foot 4½ inches of me in his direction, grabbed him by his battledress and thundered, 'I say so and YOU will put it out'. Which he did. A few weeks later in May 1942, we were on Exercise Tiger and had marched thirty-five miles starting off at 0200 and stopping at 2200. Rations had been limited to hard tack and water and there was plenty of grumbling in the ranks. 'For God's sake, shut up' I yelled, 'you'll be fed at 0500 hrs.' And then to my surprise another voice boomed forth, 'The big 'un says you'll be fed at 0500 hrs and you WILL be fed at 0500 hrs. SO SHUDDUP! It was Donald O'Connell and since the fire episode we'd developed a sort of understanding . He was the mortar man; we both marched at the rear and I'd been spelling him occasionally with the thirty-two pound mortar.

"In June 1942 all Second Division officers who could be released were brought together at a large movie house in Brighton. On arrival we learned that we'd be addressed by General Montgomery GOC-in-C South Eastern Command. This was four months prior to El Alemein. I shall never forget his truly amazing performance that day. The shortish sparely-built officer stepped briskly to centre stage, glanced at his watch, and then stated in his direct clipped manner that he would give us exactly five minutes to cough, talk, and do whatever we had to do. After that he would be speaking to us for exactly fifty-five minutes during which there'd be no sound of any sort. We'd be allowed to relax again as soon as he'd finished. Well, not in a theatre or anywhere else have I ever seen anyone command such riveted and fascinated attention. He spoke without notes putting his points over clearly and precisely. I was to hear him address troops on two later occasions but not to the galvanizing effect experienced in Brighton."

While with the Calgary Highlanders Lt. Ignatieff was sent to Chemical Warfare (CW) School for two weeks. Soon afterwards Lt-Col W.R. Sawyer, the Canadian head of CW was looking for people with chemical and military background, and Ignatieff was a likely candidate. At the time of the Dieppe raid in August 1942, he was at the main British CW establishment at Porton, near Salisbury. An intensive course there was followed by research work.

"Next I was appointed Chemical Warfare Officer for the 1st Canadian Corps and reported to General Crerar. I spent three weeks with the 3rd Division who were training at Inverary for landing operations. I used my French with the Chaudiéres and enjoyed the company of their 2 i/c (Second in Command), Major Hugues Lapointe. Meat was scarce in Britain and up there in the Scottish countryside the Chaudiéres were known to dispatch a few grazing sheep with what they referred to as 'un peu de Bren'.

With 9th Brigade on the Isle of Bute I was requested to provide a tremendous smoke screen for a particular exercise. Each smoke pot weighed forty pounds or so and we used nearly twenty tons. Outside of naval operations, a smoke screen was a rare sight then and ours was quite an event being a mile in length and of an hour's duration. I learned later that the girls on office staff got the idea that Ignatieff must be the code word for smoke."

"In October 1943 Captain Ignatieff was off to Sicily and then to Italy as Technical Officer (CW) at 1st Canadian Corps Headquarters. He travelled a great deal going from unit to unit as his services were required.

"During the Hitler Line fighting I had with me a squadron

of Royal Canadian Dragoons who were trained as smoke troops ready to work immediately behind the front line. As we moved up a large number of our wounded passed us from the opposite direction. They were laid across Jeeps, three to a vehicle. We came on more wounded being treated at a forward dressing station and on the ground nearby there lay these human parcels, about ten of them set in a row, neatly wrapped and tagged in army blankets. God, they look too small to have been men, was my impression. And I see them still.

"That same night Major Jean Prosper Gauthier, the Squadron Commander and I had gone ahead and I was taking my turn watching for our men. In the light of frequent flashes I saw a column of soldiers advancing in smart order.... and by God, they weren't ours.... they were Germans! I froze behind a large tree trying to decide on the best course to follow. Then the tension broke and I relaxed. The two soldiers bringing up the rear were Canadians!

"It was in June 1945 that my Mentioned in Dispatches (MID) was recorded in the London *Gazette*. The citation was addressed to 'Captain' Ignatieff and I believe it was awarded for my work in Italy."

On 28 December 1944 Captain Ignatieff left the Italian theatre for North-West Europe.

"On board ship the British Lt-Colonel put me in charge of troop discipline. Liquor was forbidden but as we anchored in Gibraltar harbour I guessed there was some drinking going on.

Standard Armed Forces Christmas Card.

"We had a detachment of British FANYs (Female Auxiliary Nursing Yeomenry) with us in their own section. A small concentration of womanhood among thousands of men. Late in the evening I was keeping an eye on things when a tall handsome young lieutenant lurched from somewhere and made for the women's corridor. As he opened one of the cabin doors and leaned in, I grabbed him by the seat of his pants, told him he was drunk, and to go and sleep it off. He staggered away only to reappear at intervals until I became furious and decided to read the riot act to his brother officers. 'If he turns up there again, I'll put him on charge' I warned them, 'and that could mean a court-martial which would reflect on you and your unit.' I saw no further wandering by the lurcher or anyone else that night.

"Next morning I was on deck when the young lieutenant asked permission to speak with me. He thanked me for what I'd done the previous night. There were certain times in the army when I felt I was playing the parent role."

In mid-March 1945 Major Ignatieff was appointed one of six Combined Intelligence Objective Sub-Committee CIOS Group Leaders in an organization commonly referred to as 'CW and Task Force'. Within 21 Army Group Headquarters and under the command of Brigadier G.H. Pennycook, the organization was responsible for army and navy technical intelligence and related matters.

As Group 6 Leader, Major Ignatieff headed a team of a dozen experts with particular responsibility for investigating matters concerned with chemical warfare, chemical and petroleum industries, and medicine.

By late March the Task Force teams crossed the Rhine behind the Allied forces. In spite of having seen bomb-damaged cities in Britain and the effects of intense action in Italy, the major was shocked at the vast amount of destruction in the Ruhr.

"The Allied air forces had certainly wrought devastation. The next two or three weeks I was busy on the road. What impressed me was that the smaller towns and villages were hardly touched; it was the bigger places, and particularly the industrial centres, that got the pasting. It was just the opposite to the experience in Italy where many of the smaller towns for which we fought in our advance had been badly shattered by shell-fire or bombing and the countryside in certain areas was badly seared."

By April he was aware that an important CW target existed near Münster in Lower Saxony. There was anxiety in case retreating Germans should destroy CW ammunition dumps. British forces were nearing the area and such action could have a devasting effect on forward troops, the civilian population, and the environment.

At short notice and because his troops were already spread thinly, the C.O. Münster area declined to lend a detachment to investigate the CW installation at Münsterlager. And the officer had no idea whether it was still in enemy hands.

"We had not heard any firing on that particular morning. I also knew that in some areas German troops were surrendering easily. In my travels I had seen towns and villages with white flags fluttering, and convoys of our trucks packed with prisoners travelling at great speed to prison cages. So I decided that we should investigate Münsterlager without outside help, and we went there, just we three officers and our drivers."

The officers proceeded to examine the enemy compound. They looked over residential buildings, storehouses, and laboratories where the workers had vacated minutes before (returning later) leaving their notebooks lying open. Major Ignatieff ordered the senior Warrant Officer (there were no commissioned officers on the premises) to instruct the seventy German soldiers to pile arms and consider themselves prisoners of war.

"We went into what looked like a largish barn in the general perimeter of the establishment and found the concrete floor perfectly clean. We saw a trapdoor and went down by stairway to an underground chamber, which on closer examination we concluded was a pilot plant of some sort. It was concrete, spotlessly clean, with furnaces, condensers and much tubing, all in metal.

... Later investigation by Allied scientists showed this to have been a pilot plant for production of 'Tabun', a colourless, odorless and tasteless nerve gas which could penetrate our gas respirators. Of course, at the time we did not know what kind of a pilot plant it was, but we felt it was important and were impressed by the camouflage. In the meantime our medical officer had found cabinets full of slides showing the effects of various CW gases on human organs.

... In the Canadian and British Armed Forces we had been concentrating on the possible use of Nitrogen Mustard, a persistent blister gas. We suspected the Germans of having it, but we had no idea that they had developed the Tabun nerve gas, though only up to the pilot plant stage."

After completing six months of challenging and vital operations, Major Ignatieff turned over the leadership of Group 6 in early September.

> A personal comprehensive Memoir by Major (SR, ret'd) V.P. Ignatieff. *Canadian Defence Quarterly,* Summer, 1982.

"The first conference of the Food and Agriculture Organization of the United Nations was scheduled for Quebec in October. I was about to begin a new career. Lester B. Pearson, 'Mike' thought I was right for the job.

"He saw to it that I was seconded to External Affairs. Boarding the next ship from England to Halifax, I went straight to Toronto to see my wife and children for the first time in four years. Two days later I was whisked down to Washington and then to Quebec. Assisted by men of the Royal 22e Regiment and an army of secretaries, I was Officer of the Day when FAO was formed on 16 October 1945. There were only forty countries represented at the first meeting where Boyd-Orr was elected Director General. Following my demobilization he sent me all over the world on FAO assignments."

When the FAO moved its heaquarters from Washington to Rome the Ignatieffs went along and were to spend fifteen busy years based in the Eternal City before Vladimir Ignatieff, Deputy Director of the Land and Water Development Division of FAO in the final five years, retired.

"At one point Canada's General Burns passed through Rome on his way to take command of the United Nations Forces in the Middle East. The Deputy Director of FAO went out to the airport to see whether he needed anything. General Burns sent his regards to me, informing my superior that at 1st Canadian Corps I'd been known as The Mad Russian."

Vladimir and **Florence Ignatieff** returned to Canada and now live in tranquil countryside at Richmond, Quebec, very close to where his parents had settled in 1936.

9

Sister, Who Cares?

Lieutenant Nursing Sister **Georgie Rideout,** Royal Canadian Army Medical Corps, 1943. Georgie was a Moncton girl who had taught for two years in a one-room schoolhouse in Coverdale, New Brunswick before taking that first step on the long road to Berlin.

It was late May 1945 and my cousin, Max MacLoggan (Forestry Corps) and his CWAC wife had driven me to Berlin where we'd gone straight to the ruins of Hitler's Chancellory. We were not permitted to see the rear of the building and it has always intrigued me as to whether the remains of Adolf and Eva were still on the premises.

"As I chipped a piece of marble from Hitler's already damaged desk, I was thinking – so this is where that mad paperhanger sat and planned his diabolical deeds. And then I helped myself to two of his cigars from a desk drawer.

"That evening we went to a British Officers Club. The mood was jubilant, everyone singing and dancing. And when the German band played "God Save the King", we all stood extra tall there in the heart of Berlin. But then my tears rolled – for all the thousands of young men who'd died for freedom and made it possible for me to be there on that memorable evening."

Georgina Rideout was nineteen when she went into training at Toronto General Hospital. It was the month that Canada declared war, September 1939.

Georgie Rideout and an unidentified officer on the steps of the Chancellory ruins in Berlin in May 1945. To their right is Hitler's bomb-damaged chair which was put on public view.

"Walking down Yonge Street one day, I spotted an army nursing sister in uniform; and gaping in admiration I followed her into a store; I was becoming obsessed with the idea of joining up myself. My blood boiled when I read the long lists of Canadian casualties at Dieppe and as soon as I graduated in 1943, I was off to Saint John to join the Royal Canadian Army Medical Corps.

"Following basic training in Sussex and a few months duty at St. James Military Hospital, I was posted overseas as a reinforcement. The thrill of my life! The patients at the hospital

Georgie Rideout was interviewed by a war correspondent.

The German Army in retreat in August 1944 as photographed by the nurses.

presented me with a black lace nightgown for luck – their good-natured imitation of a similar gesture in an American film featuring patients and nurses on Corregidor and Bataan. I thanked them and apologized for not looking more like Jane Wyman.

"We boarded the *Cavina* and left Halifax on 4 January 1944. I was sure that we were being ferried out to a bigger vessel but not so, the *Cavina* took her place in the convoy. We had 108 Nursing Sisters and 36 officers aboard and the small ship was packed.

"Some of the N/Ss got me out of bed one night with a request. I threw on the black lace nightgown over my long drawers and went with them. In the bar I stood on a table and sang my party piece. 'Queenie, Queen of them all'. I did not drink and it was all in good fun.

"Taking off our long drawers on the voyage was forbidden lest we were attacked by U boats. After two weeks I could stand it no longer so I drew a tub of salt water, jumped out of my Stanfields and into the tub. A quick dip and I reversed the procedure. I swear the long drawers had stood at attention for those few seconds!

"A new aircraft carrier stayed on our port side for the two and a half weeks it took to cross the Atlantic. As a joke, towards the end of the trip, I put a notice on the bulletin board: ALL THOSE INTERESTED IN GOING TO A DANCE ON THE AIR-CRAFT CARRIER TONIGHT, PLEASE SIGN BELOW. Over 100 nurses and 36 officers signed!

"I was posted to No. 16 Canadian General Hospital (CGH) at Marston Green, near Birmingham. Casualties were arriving from Italy. One remarkable patient had lost both legs and each day I'd carry him around the ward to sit him on some other soldier's bed. He would encourage and cheer up men with less serious wounds.

"In late May 1944, I was sent to No. 2 CGH at Bramshott as a reinforcement. D Day was approaching and we kept the rows of waiting beds warm with hot water bottles....

"By 7 June, the endless line of ambulances had begun delivering the wounded. No. 2 CGH was acting as a Casualty Clearing Station. On D Day plus 2, Matron asked me if I'd mind taking a shift on the prisoner-of-war ward. They were not

Canadian Casualty
Clearing Station in
Holland.

Medical Corps
personnel line up to
wash their dishes.

my favourite patients to say the least. The hatred fostered by
years of war was intense and we glared at one another
unrelentingly.

"Our own training for the continent had begun and we
went north for route marches in the Yorkshire countryside.
Along the tracks of the train ride back south, the wonderful
British people cheered us on the 'V' signs.

"In August 1944, I walked into Normandy at Courseulles
from a landing craft. A muddy two weeks under canvas at

Bayeux followed and during that time we saw some of the devastation in the invasion area. St. Lo was flattened, literally. At Coutances – which I shall always call Cow Dances – there was an odd sight. A poor old cow had been blown high into a tree and still hung there.

"From Bayeux we moved to St. Omer where the Germans may well have heard us coming for the troops had left hurriedly in mid-meal. While in St. Omer, Matron asked me to 'Special' a brigadier who had a chest condition. Inhalation treatments meant that his bed was entirely covered by a large sheet. Reaching outside for bedside table, his hand inadvertedly met my knee. 'Sister, you've got water on the knee' he quipped and I finished the old joke with 'Yes, that's why I wear pumps' and we both had a good laugh. Laughter was so very important for morale.

"Another nursing sister and I were assigned to accompany the brigadier back to his unit at the front and the press were out to meet the two nurses who happened to come from the opposite coasts of Canada. The evening before the return flight found us having dinner at the leave centre in the Brussels Hotel. Two very young officers asked whether they might talk with us. Their eyes filled as they explained that they'd just come out of hell and after their forty-eight hour leave, they'd be going right back in. I've often wondered what happened to those two handsome soldiers of the South Saskatchewan Regiment.

"While Calais and Boulogne were being attacked and Dunkirk was under siege, we were worked to our limits day and night, admitting over 2000 casualties in two weeks.

"Another move and then came my big chance; volunteers were needed for forward units. Next morning I said my goodbyes and off I went to No. 3 Canadian Casualty Clearing Station in Holland where the personnel were living under canvas and working in an old castle at Lochem. Four years ago I went to see that old castle again. Another Canadian had been there just before me. The veteran told the curator that as a wounded soldier patient, he'd nearly died there in the war. As with me, nostalgia had drawn him back.

"From his stretcher at Lochem, I remember a sergeant looking up at me with surprise and pleasure on his face. 'Why, Sister' he exclaimed, 'You're a Canadian girl! And you've got lipstick on!' It meant a lot to our fighting men to see their countrywomen over there.

"After working in Bad Zwischenhan and Oldenburg I moved up to Friesoythe, Germany. What a sight that place was! The town had been burned down and No. 6 Field Dressing Station took over an old convent, the solitary building still usable. Right across the road was a Canadian cemetery where rows and rows of new crosses marked the graves of our recent dead.

"He was only nineteen, this one patient of mine at Friesoythe. Outwardly, his wounds were not noticeable but inside his savaged body a battle for life was being won or lost. He asked me if I'd please write a letter to his mother – but just then I was called to the operating room. 'As soon as I come back' I promised him. On return the bed was empty. In the short time I'd been gone to assist in saving another life, the young soldier had died. I was so shocked I came near to fainting. And I kept thinking of his dear mother, and what that letter would have meant to her and the family. It still affects me.

"Another soldier was in a room by himself. He had a huge abdominal wound, he'd lost both legs and an arm, and he was blinded in both eyes. In that room it took a tremendous effort to keep his spirits up and my own as well. I tried but my heart ached so much for him.

"After listening to Churchill's speech announcing the cessation of hostilities, I took a sponge bath with a ration of water in my steel helmet. Then I went on duty, alone. Most of the unit had moved and being a reinforcement, I stayed behind with patients who could not be moved.

"At the start of the duty I went to the bed of one patient with 'Private, the war is over.' He looked straight at me and spoke three most poignant words. 'Sister, who cares!' He was paralyzed from the waist down and would never walk again. Sacrifices such as his can never be measured.

"Yes, 8 May 1945, VE Day, I can never forget. I had twenty-five of these seriously wounded men in my care. Six of them died in my arms that very day. The dreaded telegrams would be arriving at their homes in Canada just as most Canadians would be rejoicing over Victory in Europe.

"Off duty the next day, I walked down the road among the charred ruins of Friesoythe thinking, I'm in the only country that isn't celebrating today. And after my own very recent heart-rending experiences, I was in no mood for celebration, either."

> The normally high-spirited Lt. N/S **Georgie Rideout** sailed for home on the *Ile de France* in November, 1945. She married the fiance she had met years earlier when in teacher training in New Brunswick. Flight Lieutenant Murray Seeley had spent his war years as a Navigator, serving overseas with the RCAF and the RAF. The couple make their home in Fergus, Ontario.

10

Guns and Mud and Luck

Two brothers from Mansonville, Quebec served together for five years in the 14th Field Regiment, Royal Canadian Artillery. Eighteen-year-old **Merton E. Bailey** was fresh out of school and off the farm when he joined the 66th Field Battery in Montreal on 4 July 1940. Five weeks later his older brother, **Wilson E. Bailey** had also signed up.

A YEAR AFTER their enlistment, Gunner M.E. Bailey, wireless operator, and Gunner W.E. Bailey, driver-mechanic, were on the *Empress of Canada* bound for Britain. It was a typical troopship crossing of the time and included a U boat scare.

The brothers' three years in Britain, spent mostly in Surrey and Sussex, involved a good deal of work on firing ranges, and in due time, specific training and preparations for D Day. Mud dogged their footsteps, their vehicles, and their guns, for much of their time overseas. Like most veterans who prefer to recall the lighter moments, Merton Bailey recounts these anecdotes.

"To surprise an English girl friend I decided to take ballroom dancing lessons in a studio over The Black Horse pub in Horsham. I was the only Canadian in the class. The teacher was an older lady, about 6 foot 6 inches – anyway she was tall, and a terrific dancer. Even if you had two left feet Beryl Monro Higgs could teach you to dance. After the course of lessons ended I took the English girl to a dance and confidently swung her on to the floor. But the rest was a disaster, all stumble and trip and embarrassment for she couldn't follow my fancy new steps at all. We had to do some serious practising in her dining room before we danced in public again.

"In June 1942, I was off to Edinburgh on leave. I'd checked into a hostel and spent time getting myself smartly turned out in shirt, tie, shoes, leather gloves, etc. I hadn't gone ten feet on the street when I was picked up by MPs for impersonating an officer. Tunic open to the second button! They cancelled my leave and sent me back south. Sheepishly I went before Colonel Griffin who said he thought I'd been punished enough and let me off with a reprimand. Later, my troop commander interceded on my behalf and I got my ten days leave back. I went to Glasgow!"

The Baileys still chuckle over one of the unforgettable characters in their outfit. Albert Brouillette ran his own barbering business, charged a shilling a haircut and all the men were familiar with his most prized of possessions, the small leather satchel that contained his barbering tools. A WWI veteran, Al was in his forties and held the rank of lance-bombadier without pay in charge of sanitation. He knew his way around and sometimes this benefitted the gunners.

COMPOSITE RATION PACK

TYPE F

(14 men for one day)

Contents and Suggested Use

BREAKFAST	Tea	* 3 tins (2 tall, 1 flat—Tea, Sugar & Milk Powder)
	Luncheon Meat	3 tins
	Biscuit	* 1 tin
	Margarine	* 1 tin

(* Items marked thus are also to provide for other meals)

DINNER	Preserved Meat	12 tins
	†Vegetables (¾ hr.)	4 tins (2 large, 2 small)
	†Pudding (1 hr.)	3 tins (2 large, 1 small)
TEA	Tea	— (* see above)
	Biscuit	— (* see above)
	Margarine	— (* see above)
	Salmon	3 tins
	Jam	1 tin
SUPPER	†Soup, Scotch Broth (1 hr.)	2 tins (mix with equal quantity of water)
	Biscuit	— (* see above)
EXTRAS	Cigarettes	2 tins (1 round, 1 flat)
	Sweets	2 tins
	Salt	— { packed in one of
	Matches	— { the sweet tins
	Chocolate	1 tin (1 slab per man)
	Latrine Paper	
	Soap	1 tablet

DIRECTIONS

Tea, Sugar and Milk Powder.—Use a dry spoon and sprinkle powder on heated water and bring to boil, stirring well. 3 heaped teaspoonfuls to 1 pint of water.

† May be eaten hot or cold. To heat, place unopened tins in boiling water for minimum period as indicated. Pudding, cut into ½-inch slices, may be fried (using margarine) if preferred.

Wt. 45207/5856   310m in 7 Sorts   1/43   KJL/3605/4   Gp. 698/3
Wt. 13467/6296   84m   5/43   KJL/5275   Gp. 689/3   J.6397

"When we were in Nissen huts at Summer's Place the other huts were always short of hot water but we had it twenty-four hours a day," recalls Merton Bailey. "Al somehow scrounged the extra coal or coke that kept our boiler going. One day an officer stalked into the hut demanding to speak to someone with a little authority. Up spoke Al. 'That's me. I've got as little authority as anybody,' he quipped."

Wilson Bailey, a self-appointed well-patronized unofficial banker, kept an account book. It shows that in England he loaned out numerous amounts ranging from five shillings to ten pounds, including sundry sums to his brother.

An incident that happened on the Alfriston ranges still amuses him. It concerned an officer nicknamed Wild Bill.

"He had these young green officers up there learning how to shoot. They weren't doing very well and Wild Bill said 'You see those sheep over there,' indicating three or four sheep standing in a corner of a field. They looked, he gave the orders, the gunners fired, and the sheep disappeared. He'd got 'em square. 'Now that's what you call shooting' he told the admiring greenhorns. What they didn't realize was that it was highly doubtful that he'd have been able to duplicate such accuracy if he'd tried again. The session ended there."

By 1943 training became increasingly arduous. They went from one firing camp to another in southern England, then to Wales for more shooting in more rain and mud. In July a contingent of officers and other ranks left for instruction on tank equipment and maintenance. Gunner Wilson Bailey was among them. Two weeks of intense Combined Operations work came next. The decisive training prior to D Day, 6 June 1944, was done from Christchurch, Hants in close conjuction with naval forces. It consisted of amphibious exercises, lectures on assault landings, waterproofing of vehicles, and gun calibrating.

Gunner Wilson Bailey added tank driver to his qualifications, the regiment now being temporarily equipped with Sherman tanks carrying Self-Propelled 105 mm guns. Gunner Merton Bailey was designated co-driver and expected to handle ammunition in addition to operating his field radio.

"After a certain amount of training, I was permitted to drive one of the guns during a convoy exercise. We had to cross a

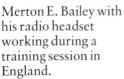

Merton E. Bailey with his radio headset working during a training session in England.

Beach obstacles set up by the Germans hindered the Canadian invasion forces at Bernières-sur-Mer, 6 June 1944.

bridge while passing a convoy coming in the opposite direction. I thought I was doing fine but once across the bridge, the officer in charge stopped us and informed me that I had side-swiped several vehicles. I was immediately grounded for a few days and incidentally, never drove a tank in convoy again."

From their final camp in England, near Portsmouth, the brothers went aboard their LCT (Landing Craft Tank) at Southhampton. Merton Bailey tells about his experiences before and on D Day.

"Hundreds of boxes, each containing forty-four pounds of ammunition, had to be loaded on to the LCT. It would be fired into the beach area to help soften up defences for the infantry assault. A lot of us did a hard afternoon's work on 4 June.

"On 5 June our ships and craft sailed out to the Solent and into the English Channel to join others gathering from all directions. Sealed orders were opened and then we knew for sure that this was the big show. We sailed on towards France.

"I don't recall feeling nervous or frightened at that stage. Excited to some extent, yes. Thousands of aircraft were streaming overhead on their way to bomb German defences. And around us, as far as we could see, ships.

"Once out of the harbour area, the sea became very choppy and I became very sick. I lay down on the rim of the LCT and stayed there all night wishing that someone would kick me overboard. About 0500 hrs someone did kick me. It was the sergeant-major. 'Get up,' he ordered, 'we're preparing to fire,' I moaned that I was too ill. No use of course. So there I was, about to invade France and so sick I could hardly stand up.

"Somehow I set about my job of handing up the rounds of ammunition from the deck to the gunners in the SP gun. At 0730 we started into firing drive, adding our shells to all the others raining on coastal targets at Bernières-sur-Mer. After

The 14th Field Regiment, Royal Canadian Artillery, in northern Europe.

close to half an hour and as planned, we withdrew further off-shore and the infantry went in to clear the beach of obstacles (some of which were mined) and to breach the sea wall. Owing to the rough seas, our firing hadn't been as effective as hoped. But it was time to throw all extra loose ammunition overboard and clear the way for SP guns' exit from the LCT. Wilson had driven the first tank aboard so he'd be last off. The lucky son of a gun hadn't been seasick at all.

"As we went back in, this time to land, I was hit with what war was about. There were dead soldiers floating in the water, others lying where they'd fallen on the beach, and clusters of wounded waiting for help. Shelling was heavy and steady.

"Our waterproofed tanks performed well but owing to a traffic jam at the single opening in the sea wall, we were held up on the beach. And while we waited we were sitting ducks. Hell all around us and we stayed lucky. Wilson's tank was temporarily caught on a trap but again, no harm done.

"On into and through Bernières-sur-mer and our luck was holding. I was in D Troop, 66th Field Battery and we were scheduled to go into this certain field on the right side of the road. Because we'd been delayed at the sea wall, two SPs from A Troop and one from C Troop had been directed into that field in our place. They were no sooner in there than German 88 mm guns picked them off. The 88's emplacement was hidden in a field of wheat. Heavy casualties resulted and the ammunition and debris exploded and burned for hours.

"We moved on and took up gun positions in an orchard on the left side of the road, overlooking Beny-sur-Mer. Thus far still no casualties in our Troop but the Battery had had many. My wireless was is operation and at noon dozens of prisoners of war were passing our location. By evening we moved on again and took up positions in a wheat field. That first night was more scary to me than the landing. There was thunder and lightning, cloud and moonlight, and bombing and shelling that went on all night. We were detailed one at a time, to stand guard in front of our guns, relieved as I remember after one hour. Still in our baptism of fire, and with the awful noise and the waving wheat adding to the eeriness, it was easy to imagine that German patrols were sneaking up from this or that direction. Presumably our infantry was ahead but the lines were fluid at that early stage, to say the least."

From the history of the 14th Field Regiment on that first night: The night was sleepless as there was constant shelling and it was all so new to the green gunners that sleep was out of the question. In this position were dug the first slit trenches and command posts.

On the next night, 7 June, Wilson Bailey found himself a haystack and slept soundly.

"The rest of the crew slept inside the tank but my driver's seat would have meant me sitting bolt upright all night – so I took the haystack in spite of rain and shelling. A German patrol was in the vicinity and I woke briefly once to the sound of small arms fire. Some time in the night another Canadian had crawled under the haystack and at daybreak we found a couple of dead Germans nearby."

Then the brothers did not see one another for about ten days. Bombadier Wilson Bailey and his Sherman had been off in support of the Stormont, Dundas and Glengarry Highlanders.

CANADIANS

You are again to assume the offensive. In case you should come into a hopeless situation don't lose courage. Germany treats prisoners of war according to the Hague and Geneva conventions. Your soldier's honour will be respected

BETTER COME ACROSS
THAN GET A CROSS

ARE CANADIANS COWARDS ?

Never has anybody dared to assert that. Even Canada's enemies rank Canadians among the world's best soldiers.

AND YET

more than 6500 out of 16.000 newly drafted Canadians have deserted bevore the embarkation to Europe, stated Minister of Defence Mac Naughton officially. Are these 6500 boys cowards? No. They simply ran away to return to their families and to work. They see no point in fighting in Europe, fighting with Bolshevism as allied. They rather see that all over Canada, in fam ring as well as in the lumber business, labour is lacking, men are wanted, production slackens.

MEN WANTED TO USE DYNAMITE FOR PEACEFUL PURPOSE
Acres of floating logs — next to grain, Canada's most important harvest. Often jams occur, clogging a river, and then logmen entangle upturned logs. With the aid of long, spike-ended poles, and sometimes dynamite, they start them on their voyage to distant mills.

"I was exhausted after that. Moving a lot, always on edge with hardly any sleep. On the final night I went with Captain Buchanan to a First Aid Station where the doctor gave me a pill saying, 'This will make you sleep for a couple of hours, then you're on your own.' I laid down right there on the hard wooden floor with a blanket over me and my boots and tunic for a pillow. When I came to I'd slept over twelve hours."

Merton Bailey recalls that during that same period, he was driving around the bridgehead.

"We'd move all over the place, firing here and there. I believe it was to make Jerry think that more artillery and armour had landed than actually had."

He remembers guns firing in awesome unison near Caen.

"We shot hundreds of rounds and in the distance all you could see was a vast panorama of smoke and dust where all the shells were landing. For all I know the whole brigade or even all the guns in the army could have been firing then. It was a hellish noise that seemed as if it would never end. My hearing was never as good afterwards."

In early August the unit had been re-issued with field artillery. From a slit trench near the village of Cauvicourt, he watched in horror as a costly error by Allied bombers resulted in heavy Canadian and Polish casualties. The planes were engaged in carpet bombing prior to a ground attack designed to break through south and south-east of Caen.

"Up close to the front, we were watching these heavy bombers as they roared in from the rear. The first wave dropped their cargo ahead of us; the second wave hadn't reached our position when bomb doors opened and the bombs began falling. It was so shocking that you refused to believe it at first. The earth was shaking violently and I was sure that the slit trench would collapse. Remarkably, it held. Again, it was a miracle that no-one in our outfit was hurt; many of our vehicles were damaged or destroyed.

"I had an even narrower escape during the battle for Boulogne. I had just left my little tent (two German groundsheets fastened together) to go forward with the Battery Commander as his wireless operator, when an enemy shell landed on our position. My tent, bedroll, and the rest of my possessions were riddled by shrapnel.

"As our convoys went through French towns, people would come out and greet us by throwing flowers. Later, in Holland we'd see pale thin children rooting in garbage. And when we'd get ready to eat they'd stand and stare, eyes begging for something to eat. You never forget that.

"The most despicable thing I saw was at a convent where we slept overnight, just inside Germany I think. The stripped bodies of several nuns lay outside and they'd been deliberately and horribly mutilated. We never found out who did it or why.

"At the Scheldt Estuary our trucks and guns were often bogged down. Guns had to be hauled up on to dykes, the only solid ground. Your feet and boots were wet for days on end. It rained and rained. We'd go to bed soaking wet and get up the same way and that was where I had my first bronchial asthma attack."

Between the numerous halts to contribute fire-power in battle actions, the 14th Field Regiment had made its way from the Normandy bridgehead, across north-west Europe, into Germany. Along the nerve-shatteringly noisy and bloody route, nearly 200 of its officers and men had been killed or wounded.

It was on 4 May 1945, his twenty-third birthday, that Gunner Merton E. Bailey received the historic message CEASE FIRE UNLESS FIRED UPON over his field telephone. It was immediately relayed to the guns over the loud-speaker system. The final CEASE FIRE order came the following morning.

Wilson Bailey, ex-farmer, still lives in Masonville, Quebec. **Merton Bailey**, following thirty-one years with the Department of National Revenue, Customs and Excise Division, lives in retirement at nearby Highwater, Quebec.

11

With First Overseas Draft

of the CWACS

Irene M. Vivash and her friend, Alice Pruner, had left assembly line jobs at Westclox Canada in Peterborough, Ontario when they joined up. From December 1941 until July 1946, Irene served in the Canadian Women's Army Corps, a force which numbered over 20,000 by the war's end. For her it was a hectic and busy time during which she rose from the rank of private to Warrant Officer II, Quartermaster-Sergeant. Her dedication to duty was recognized with the award of the British Empire Medal.

CWAC SERVICE WAS to bring her friendships, opportunities, and hardship. She tells about many aspects of that life.

"In World War I, my father had tried to enlist, first in England and then in Canada but was turned down in both countries. My brother tried early in WWII and he too, was declared medically unfit. Thus, I had a strong urge to represent the family in the Canadian Forces and four months after the Corps was authorized, I signed up. My friend Alice had a soldier fiance, and two brothers overseas in the Canadian Army.

"In the beginning our only item of uniform was a red armband bearing the initials CWAC and worn over the sleeve of civilian clothing. In the bare cold armouries of Gananoque, we drilled in a variety of winter clothes. There were huge fur collars, silly hats, and click-clicking fashionable high heels that outnumbered sensible brogues. Alice marched in front of me and her silver fox fur piece flipped up and hit me in the face each time the sergeant-major called Halt – causing me to sneeze, her to giggle, and the sergeant-major to bellow. What a cross-section of life we represented but we quickly learned to put aside prejudices and soon become friends with girls from very different backgrounds to our own.

"You got used to being called by your surname only. And to the harsh discipline. You were never asked if you could or would, it was *Do* this or *I* want this or that done. You learned patience and tolerance, to accept the inevitable, and to queue for most everything. A sense of humour became a prime necessity. You discovered that you could survive without privacy and you found yourself doing all sorts of menial tasks, no protests allowed. Your bedroom was a cubicle of stark walls and bare scrubbed floors. Folded grey blankets and heavy grey sheets lay on top of the mattress ticking. Helmets, gas mask, and haversacks had their place and your barrack box was stowed beneath the bed. The coloured curtain which hung in place of a door to the hall, was your one chance to express individuality. At times it seemed close to a prison situation but together with the plain living went the warm sense of companionship, the joy of shared loyalties, pride of purpose, and plenty of fun and laughter.

"The day we graduated we wore our new uniforms (to us the smartest of the women's services), dreaded the requisite

97

army haircut, and began worrying about making foolish saluting errors.

"Four of us, Alice and I included, were sent to the old permanent force barracks at Fort Frontenac, Kingston. We'd heard that 'the old man', Colonel Hughes, had vowed that he was not having any of those women soldiers in HIS camp. Under protest he relented enough to allow four scared recruits in – with the proviso that they proved themselves in a couple of weeks or there'd be no more. To make matters worse, Alice was chosen for the lion's den (Colonel Hughes Office) and I was slated for the Documents Office under an officer known to the men as a terror. Pitiful looks were cast my way when soldiers found out I'd be working for Captain William Grey. They'd give me two or three days at the most. But they were wrong. The presence of a woman actually helped; the Captain mellowed, the men's work improved and their 'cussing' was modified. This was repeated wherever the CWACs were posted and instead of 'Don't send us any of those women' it soon became 'When the hell are we going to get those CWACs you promised us?'. (In the book *Duffy's Regiment* by Kenneth B. Smith, Regimental Sergeant-Major Angus Duffy is quoted on the CWAC. 'They were tremendously good soldiers and a credit to Canada.' And according to Irene Vivash, 'No one but no one ever questioned Duffy!'.)

"The clothing allowance to purchase our own lingerie was withdrawn when we were drafted overseas. Displayed on long wooden tables in a large warehouse there were khaki and beige panties, slips, pyjamas, and even army issue bras and girdles. And at the end we found those horrors of horrors, long drawers and undervests. The sight provoked comments such as 'we have to take them but we don't have to wear them' and 'I wouldn't be caught dead in them.' But before long we came to appreciate the underwear and wished that the girls back home realized its warmth and comfort.

"Among the first draft of 100 CWAC (hand-picked from across the country), I went overseas in the fall of 1942. I would spend almost two years working in London where our barracks was the former home of Lord and Lady Abercrombie on South Street. We were required to take our turns on fire picquet duty and while some nights were peaceful, others were terrifying. You'd stand on a roof during an alert scanning the sky, watching the arcing searchlights and waiting for an enemy raider to be caught in their converging beams. Then the ack-ack guns would open up all around and you callously prayed that they'd send the Jerry plummeting earthward, or that he'd be far away when he unloaded his bombs. Never mind who got killed as long as it wasn't you. Next day you expressed your sympathy for the victims but you knew that your first thought and your 'thank God they didn't hit the barracks' were primarily for yourself.

"The sirens sounded once when I was in a London beauty salon having a permanent wave. There'd been a week of bombers' weather and nerves were becoming frayed. With my hair suspended in strands from the waving machine, I watched the establishment empty swiftly. My operator informed me that she had set the machine so I should be alright – and then she too, hurried off to shelter. I had my moment of panic picturing a bomb falling nearby and the blast hurtling me into the street, scalped. But a more immediate danger blotted out that vision for the curlers were overheating and scorching my head.

Kay Drinkwater of Orillia, Peggy Reid from Nova Scotia, and Irene Vivash of Peterborough kept accurate records.

There was no hairdresser to fan them or hold them away from my head (as they did in those days) so I just sat there in terror until the machine turned itself off. For weeks I had the frizziest head in London!

"The CWAC seemed to discourage romance. Girls like Alice waited months for the necessary permission to marry and afterwards faced the difficulty of obtaining parallel leaves. Certainly officialdom stayed clear of providing any kind of accommodation for their married personnel.

"We proved that women could keep secrets. Some CWACs worked in offices handling highly confidential information, troop movements and exercises, and early details of deaths that could not be shared. Several of us knew of the death of Alice's brother on the Italian front but we had to wait for her to get the news in a letter from her mother in Canada. Fortunately, her other brother was in London when their mother's letter arrived. Later, my friend, Alice Pruner Morin, became pregnant and was sent home from London to await the birth of her first child.

"The girls of 41 Coy were served by excellent cooks and an efficient grapevine. Although we left South Street each morning and dispersed to different offices in the city, if there was something tempting on the dinner menu we'd all find out and race back after work to enjoy it. A mutton and greens meal sent us elsewhere but eggs and bacon brought us all back to South Street.

"In a small crowd of people, one day I stood gazing at an attractive bowl of mouth-watering fruit in Fortnum and Mason's display window. We all stared as though at a famous work of art.

"While on leave in Cornwall, some of us sat around the fire one evening dreaming aloud about rum toddy. Rum was easy to get, eggs and milk were not. Next day a plan of campaign had us knocking on farm doors to chat and to casually mention how long it had been since we'd had fresh eggs or milk. That night we had our rum toddy and slept well.

"There'd been a lively air of anticipation abroad in England for weeks. Rumours flew but we knew better than to spread them further. More areas in the south were restricted. Girls hadn't heard from brothers or boyfriends for a couple of weeks and dependable men broke dates without explanation. Something big was imminent.

"Proof came on the unforgettable morning, 6 June 1944. We awoke to the steady hum of hundreds of aircraft and even before we reached the windows, we knew the invasion was on. There was excitement, pride, tears, and secret prayers – plus speculation as to when we'd be going ourselves.

"The time had come for me to leave London and its flying bomb attacks for 'the field'. In southern England, as one of only two senior NCOs, I hated walking into the Mess the first few times to the stares of around 200 men. But I was starving and it was the only place I was allowed to eat so there was no way out.

"By this time I was NCO in charge of Card Index Section, GHQ, 2nd Enchelon. We knew that our stay in England must now be limited and that as soon as the army pushed far enough inland, we'd be going across to France.

"Quickly and quietly, the whole headquarters and its equipment was loaded on to huge lorries which pulled out one morning soon after first light. It sticks in my memory because the evening before, in spite of official CB (Confined to barracks), a CWAC pal and I ignored sirens and flying bombs to join two officer friends for a wonderful last night of dining and dancing in London. It turned out that we'd really been gambling for we hadn't been back in bed for more than an hour when we heard reveille and the call to board the lorries.

"Hidden in a wooded area not far from Southampton, the staging camp – complete with street names, was a masterpiece of organization. Allied units moved in and out in orderly fashion. Quarters for Nursing Sisters, CWACs, and British counterparts were situated away from the tent streets full of men. The PA system voices went on and on announcing arrivals and departures of units, medical parades, mealtimes, etc. The camp was supervised by Americans and the rations (food we hadn't seen in years, and direct from the US) drew delighted gasps from us all. The British were in charge of the smooth-running traffic control operation.

"After two pleasant restful days a voice boomed 'Canadian Section, 2nd Echelon will form up ready to move....' and we were on our way to the docks. The ship was full of reinforcement troops going to replace the heavy casualties around Caen and Falaise. The forty or so women were supplied with state-rooms and stewards. Then women were paid less than the men; the reason given being that we required special treatment at times. So be it! The sea was calm and glassy and I stood on the afterdeck watching a glorious sunset throwing its pink and mauve reflection across the water and the ship. An accordian played and a baritone sang 'Bless This House'. I looked at all those faces turned toward that sunset and wondered how many of those quiet men would see their homes again. 'Death might come to others, never to you.'

Letter writing went on as the laundry dried, winter or summer.

"All sizes and shapes of ships greeted us in the morning and before noon we'd dropped anchor in sight of the famous floating docks installed off Avranches. Then it was into the LCI (Landing Craft Infantry) and two months after D Day, I'd landed in France. Driving along the dusty roads I noted the mute evidence of war; the graves near the roadside marked by rough crosses and sometimes a steel helmet or a rifle stuck in the ground; the broken gliders and wrecked armoured vehicles in the fields. And so we came to La Delivrande and the rows of tents in an orchard, home for the next few weeks.

" All news, supplies, and casualties were cleared through our 2nd Echelon headquarters and because of the efficient records system, the Canadian Army was able to locate very close to 100% of its personnel at any given time. Our work entailed keeping up to date the extensive card index covering every Canadian soldier, Nursing Sister, and CWAC in the European theatre. Those who went in and out of hospital; on leave; who were evacuated to field hospitals, first aid units, or general hospitals; those buried in a plot, a ditch beside the road, or in a field. It was our duty to investigate until each one was accounted for and it meant that we were as close to the front as was deemed wise. Daily trips were made to the front and many of our Jeeps did not return. News came in on hospital admittance sheets, from units as they moved or buried their dead, and occasionally from sorting through personal effects of the wounded or dead. The service number was most important in identifying one Smith or Clark from another so that the wrong family would not be notified in regard to a casualty.

"Completely mobile, our office unit of around 1000 persons, together with all equipment and records, was ready to move across the continent at very short notice. My CWAC years were spent against this background of mostly routine but unquestionably essential office work.

"The flies on the apples in the Normandy orchard gave us dysentery and a long line of victims waited in discomfort outside the Medical Officer's tent. If you had to leave your place to dash to the latrine, on your return you'd be back where you started – last in the line. Agony Row was our name for the lineups and the groans would have done justice to the great Caesar's ghost of childhood imagination.

"And then there were the night raids. Rumour had it that the Germans were trying to hit a large British camp in the vicinity and we spent more than one night in damp slit trenches. With greatcoats over pyjamas and gas capes over the coats, curlers under steel helmets, and our cream covered faces — we were hardly Hollywood-style women at war.

"Some of us were returning to camp on a pitch-black wet night, guided only by a dim flashlight in the lead. Suddenly I realized that my friend's voice was faint. She'd been close

The convoy on route to Antwerp passed mounds of rubble and many bomb-damaged buildings.

behind me but had fallen into a sodden slit trench. What was she doing down there, we asked — only to be treated to an uncharacteristic stream of cursing. When the trenches were too water-logged to be used, we'd lay on our camp beds wearing our steel helmets and praying. The tent leaked and it was often very cold. We'd get ready for bed wearing our warmest clothes, then piled other things under and over us. The weight didn't help our sleep and the groundsheet on top had to be lifted every so often to toss off the excess water. Mud was everywhere and we sure appreciated our slacks and high rubber boots.

"Between the rains, the sun appeared fitfully, we recovered from the dysentery and there were weekly parades to the beach to swim. The outdoor living was healthy even if we were cold most of the time. We made up our faces by candlepower and we attended an occasional dance held in a tent with a wet canvas dance floor. The liquor was good, the music cheered us and we could always find something to laugh about.

"At La Delivrande in Normandy, we'd walk through cultivated fields that lay between our tents and the school where we worked. The farmers' vegetables growing anywhere near the path soon disappeared. Some lucky member of the sergeants Mess would hand the cook an egg or two, and then sit eating the result. We'd pretend not to notice but secretly coveted every mouthful. For language reasons it was most often the French Canadian soldiers who'd make friends with farmers and beg or barter for produce.

"On the long convoy trip through France to Antwerp, Belgium we rode four or five to a truck, each group responsible for its own meals of iron rations cooked by canned heat. When the trucks made their specified stops it was like a Mack Sennet comedy. They halted at the required distance from the truck in front but no one moved except two men who raced across the nearest open field carrying two long poles, a length of burlap, and spades. They set up the crude screen and came back to report to our CO, Captain Marjorie Unsworth of Victoria, B.C. She'd instruct me to take the girls to the latrine and off we ran, trying not to giggle but it wasn't easy to maintain dignity in those circumstances — especially with all those men watching! We disappeared (or so we thought) behind the burlap, being careful not to stoop too low as the bottom edge was several inches above the ground. 'All together now' we said – and did our duty. Later, a friend would tell me something he thought I should know. Apparently the duffers who'd rigged the 'walls of Jericho' had it set so that the sun provided the convoy with a clear silhouette view of our operations. At another stop we occupied an old abandoned farmhouse. The ground was muddy and as you straddled the latrine trench a girl on either side held your hand to prevent you slipping into that horrible hole. Yet in spite of such trials that trip was fun.

"Into Antwerp and the CWACs hotel billet – only later to find out that we were located in the middle of the Red Light district. The townspeople mistook us for some sort of official camp followers and Belgian women pushed us around on the streets. In consequence we were transported to work in trucks, and it took a lot of explaining before the locals understood our true function in the army. Eventually we moved into the office building where we worked, a former Gestapo headquarters.

"At the time pockets of Nazis still held out in Antwerp. Dates by decree were threesomes. You, your date, and a second soldier – both men carrying rifles. Few wanted to be the odd man out. Usually a bargain was struck – I'll take you tonight if you take my girlfriend and me tomorrow night. The second escort usually got his desired goodnight kiss.

"Another problem presented itself in North-West Europe. Where could you go for privacy with a date? We had no cars or real homes; it was no fun kissing in the mess or CWAC lounge with numerous onlookers around. Some did manage to find a dark corner in an office but even for a goodnight kiss, there was a chance of being put on charge for 'conduct unbecoming'. Whenever we moved into new quarters we learned to stake out likely corners or doorways nearby. In order to get ahead of the gang you had to return early from a date and occupy your space. It was not uncommon to hear someone call out, 'Come on in here – we're leaving.' I found it amusing but demeaning, too. Our need for affection was reduced to something almost illicit.

"My worst experience as far as food was concerned was in Antwerp when our supplies were held up during the Battle of the Bulge. After weeks of runny powdered potatoes mixed

Sunday church parade, Lemgo, Germamy.

with a sloppy stew into which you threw a slice of bread, stomachs often rebelled and either a double shot of liquor was substituted or you resorted to one of the local cafés. Given the right signal, the waiter would later point to a door through which you'd slip into the kitchen for fried potatoes and some sort of meat. This cost plenty and it was against army orders to eat French fries or other fried foods. I suspect the reason was that the fat may have resulted from the rendering down of dogs and cats. The meat was almost certainly horseflesh but we suffered no ill effects.

"In Antwerp the CWAC quarters were on the top floor of the six or seven storey building. During the V1 attack on the city, we'd lay in our beds listening to the staccato approach and praying that the thing would keep on going beyond us, feeling the vibration of the building as one passed overhead. I'd linger downstairs as long as possible or if I was at the Sergeants Mess some blocks away, I'd stay there until it closed. Anything to avoid going up to the top floor nearer that dreaded doodlebug noise. But there was a saturation point and you became so exhausted that you fell asleep and another day had passed. We were fortunate in escaping serious injuries or building damage.

"Following the setback at the Scheldt, most of our staff

were evacuated to Alost. One night a German plane must have spotted our lights for he made a pass over us firing as he went. It was the worst scare we had. Shells came through the windows of the school where our night staff were working, tore through a wall leaving a gaping hole, and into the hallway where more damage was done.

"Our armies advanced and early in 1945 we moved up again. This time we rode in the bellies of transport planes and debarked in Lemgo, Germany. We were housed in former German permanent force barracks set at the foot of scenic hills. The Russians had left the buildings dirty as pigsties and the living quarters were reminiscent of the unheated armouries back home. Bare-walled, damp and musty places, no mattresses – just slats and blankets.

"I have less recollection of that period. I was still working long hours but feeling very tired, both physically and mentally. Later I found out that I had a hyper-thyroidism condition which was at least partly responsible for my exhaustion and depression. I travelled hundreds of miles to a Canadian hospital near Bremerhaven for the probable removal of an ovarian cyst. I begged to be allowed to sleep for two days but that luxury was negated at night by thousands of mosquitoes that swarmed in through the windows which had all their panes shattered. No surgery was needed and after two weeks I returned to the unit. With prescribed medication, I was able to carry on.

"Casualty figures and other statistics were still pouring in and we spent VE Day working hard to clear them. I had some difficulty in realizing that the war really was at an end for it had ruled so many of our lives so completely and for so long."

Following demobilization, **Irene Vivash** worked on the staff of *The Peterborough Examiner* until she took early retirement. She remains an active member of the Peterborough community.

Award of THE BRITISH EMPIRE MEDAL to W.3203 Staff-Sergeant (Acting Warrant Officer, Class II, Quartermaster-Sergeant) Irene Miawa VIVASH
Canadian Women's Army Corps

THIS WARRANT OFFICER, AS SUPERVISING CLERK IN CARD INDEX AND ENQUIRIES SECTION, CANADIAN SECTION 2 ECHELON, HEADQUARTERS, 21 ARMY GROUP, HAS, ON ALL OCCASIONS, PERFORMED HER DUTIES IN A MOST EXEMPLARY MANNER. THE EFFICIENCY OF THE SYSTEM OF CASUALTY REPORTING, WHICH IS CONSTANTLY BEING TESTED WITH THE UTMOST RIGOUR, IS LARGELY DUE TO HER UNTIRING VIGILANCE AND CHEERFUL LEADERSHIP OF THIS LARGE SECTION. ON MANY OCCASIONS, WHEN CASUALTIES HAVE BEEN HEAVY, SHE HAS DEVOTED LONG HOURS FAR BEYOND HER NORMAL COURSE OF DUTY, SUPERVISING DAY AND NIGHT SHIFTS IN A MANNER WHICH HAS BEEN AN INSPIRATION TO ALL RANKS ASSOCIATED WITH HER. IN ADDITION TO HER WORK SHE HAS GIVEN LEADERSHIP IN CANADIAN WOMEN'S ARMY CORPS SPORTS AND IN THIS, HAS ASSISTED GREATLY IN GUARDING THE HEALTH OF A SECTION WHOSE WORK COULD BE EASILY IMPAIRED BY THE MONOTONOUS ATTENTION TO DETAIL REQUIRED OF IT.

Quartermaster-Sergeant Irene M. Vivash with her parents following the investiture of the British Empire Medal by Viscount Alexander of Tunis at Kingston, Ontario, 6 August 1946.

12

Joking in the Face of Death

Reginald Law of Campbellton, New Brunswick is a soft-spoken and gentle man who thanks God every day of his life for his survival in prisoner-of-war camps. This picture of Reg was taken in 1940.

WHEN THEY RETURNED to Canada in 1945, ex-Hong Kong prisoners of war were unable to 'leave it all behind' and live out healthy normal lives. Many would die relatively young. And to varying degrees, the rest would go on suffering the long-term effects of physical and/or mental stress experienced as prisoners of the Japanese. For twenty-seven years following the war, Reg worked as a transport driver, but the trauma of the war years was still a handicap.

"I'd worked my way up with the CNR and then lost the job on medical grounds definitely related to POW life. My nerves were shot and I'd gone to pieces; I couldn't even drive my own car. At fifty-two and unemployed, I laid around home for eighteen months, worrying about how the family would keep going. I was a wreck and I thought the world was done with me."

With the support and understanding of his wife, Hectorine, and their three children, he recovered enough to take a job again. At first he could manage only two days a week as a commissionaire but gradually took on a full week's work.

Prior to joining the Royal Rifles of Canada in 1940, Reg Law had worked as a river guide escorting American tourists on salmon fishing expeditions in the Campbellton area. When Rifleman Reg Law sailed aboard the Prince Robert from Vancouver on 27 October 1941, he was nineteen. To their disappointment the soldiers were not allowed ashore at Pearl Harbour when the ship docked there on its way to the Far East.

"I'd got to know one of the sailors and he said that I could go up to the crows-nest so as to get a really good view of the shore. I was up there enjoying myself when I suddenly spotted one of our officers on the lower deck. If he looks up and sees me, I thought, I'm for it. On the spur of the moment I decided to dive from the crows-nest into the water. Quite a distance down! I liked diving and I'll always remember that one. It kept me out of trouble."

"When they reached Hong Kong on 16 November the Maritimer found the heat overpowering, far worse than anything he would have experienced at home. Soon, the weather was to become a lesser worry.

The Japanese first attacked Hong Kong on 7 December 1941. When the exhausted and outnumbered defenders were

ordered to surrender on 25 December, the Japanese took 5072
British, 3819 Indians, 1689 Canadians and 357 other Imperials as prisoners of war.

"Combat. It was horrible. Worse than anything I'd imagined. Although we were young raw soldiers, we had plenty of
spirit and did our best. But we were plunged into a desperate
situation for which our training had not prepared us. I have the
scars from shrapnel wounds received in the battle but I never
reported them at the time. Compared with the carnage I saw
around me, my wounds seemed insignificant."

Following capture, Reg Law became a medical orderly in
the North Point Prison Camp Hospital. He worked alongside
good-natured Fred Kelly, a fellow New Brunswicker.

"Freddy kept me going. A great boy who could joke and
make life easier even in the the worst moments. We needed
someone like him around.

"It was a terrible time. A time when we'd get up each morning and ask how many of our men had died in the night. We

Personnel of the Royal Rifles of Canada en route to Hong Kong,
Valcartier, Quebec, 23 October 1941.

orderlies had to be undertakers as well. Sometimes we'd be on burial duty and occasionally when we'd turn a corpse over, there'd be an escape of air that sounded like a sigh or moan. A new orderly offered to help one day and sure enough, it happened. Freddy didn't blink, just tapped the dead man on the shoulder and spoke sharply, 'Now you shut your mouth. There's nothing more we can do for you.' The new guy took off fast.

"Later, when we were both orderlies in the Yokahama Prison Camp Hospital, a little Japanese maid came in with a new light bulb I'd requested. When she climbed up on a chair to put it in, Freddy climbed on the chair too, patted her lightly on the bum and said, 'Reggie, isn't that something nice, eh.' I had to smile but underneath I was terrified. Thank God she took it in good part and didn't report him. If she'd told the Japanese guards, the punishment would likely have been drastic."

Reg Law was in one of the first drafts of Canadians to be shipped to Japan. From Yokohama and hospital duty, he was sent to work in the coal mines of the Sendai area.

"I was corporal in charge of a shift of men from the Royal Rifles and the Winnipeg Grenadiers. We worked ten-hour shifts on very small rations of food. You had to produce a certain amount of coal and you were allowed just so much dynamite to blast it out. If your shift didn't dig out the tonnage they'd specified that morning, they'd make you wrench and tear at the coal by hand – until the quota was filled. By this time our surviving boys were pitifully weak.

"Only three days before we got word of the Japanese surrender, I'd been badly cut on my back and arm while digging coal. A Japanese fellow put me on a trolley and took me straight up to the top for attention. I'll remember that. There were good and bad Japanese, and today I have no ill-feeling towards them."

Freed by the Americans in September 1945, the Canadians were flown to Vancouver.

Reg Law had weighed 198 pounds when captured. During internment he'd suffered pneumonia, pleurisy, dysentery and malaria. On release he was an emaciated 98 pounds of skin and bone.

"I arrived back in Canada wearing an American Navy uniform. I recall that a girl named McLean took me under her wing and sewed the badges on my new Canadian battledress. The warm welcome and generous treatment given us in Vancouver was overwhelming. After four years of degradation, just being accepted as equals again would have been great – to be fussed over was wonderful.

"On my way back I'd sent several telegrams but I'd had no news from my family. That was hard to bear. I'd given the authorities a neighbour's telephone number, hoping that he'd get hold of my mother. My father had died while I was in Newfoundland before we left for Hong Kong.

"I'd been in Vancouver a few days before there was word from the family. It turned out that they'd not known whether I was alive or dead until the news of my return to Canada eventually reached them. Cards I'd written home from prison camp had never got through and in those four years not one of the parcels they'd sent had reached me."

Little or no contact with home for four years, long hours of hard work while suffering malnutrition, extremely harsh treatment and ravages of disease, the incredible strain of watching comrades dying slowly.... thus an unbreakable bond was forged as the survivors of C Force faced the years of 'living hell' together. It is not maudlin sentimentality or a boozey haze that makes a quiet Canadian like Reg Law declare "There is not a man in the Hong Kong veterans group that I don't love."

Reg Law and his wife Hectorine remain residents of Campbellton, New Brunswick.

13

Biscuit, Book, and Candle
in Hong Kong

Lloyd Doull, a native of Atholville, New Brunswick, was a resident of Drummondville, Quebec when he joined the Royal Rifles of Canada. Lloyd, was at Camp Valcartier, Quebec weighing 155 pounds before he left for Hong Kong in September 1941. By September 1943, at Camp Niigata, Japan, Sergeant Doull weighed only 100 pounds. His prisoner-of-war number 1444 was marked on the pocket of his overalls.

Together with the Winnipeg Grenadiers, the Royal Rifles made up the Canadian C. Force. In late 1941 the Canadians were rushed across the Pacific and into the hopeless fight to defend the British Crown Colony of Hong Kong. The under-trained but determined C Force joined British and Indian garrison troops in a searing eighteen-day-long engagement against a continual onslaught of seasoned Japanese invaders.

The Canadians suffered from the lack of adequate arms and efficient deployment of manpower, from the shortage of water and food and sleep, but continued their stubborn resistance until the official surrender to the Japanese on 25 December.

Unfortunately, Sergeant Doull contracted malaria and for ten days during the siege, he was alternating between a burning 105 degrees Fahrenheit and bouts of shivering beneath his greatcoat.

"It was either the 17th or 18th December when I was carried out of the dugout on a stretcher to a forward aid post and given quinine. When the post came under heavy mortar fire the doctor said he was getting the hell out of there, I was loaded into a truck, and we drove to St. Albert's Convent Hospital.

"Following capture on the 23rd, I spent the longest and most frightening few hours of my life. Around fifteen of us were lined up, hands on top of heads, while two Japanese soldiers took turns swivelling a large machine gun back and forth. It lasted for five hours. Then for some reason they decided to spare us and we were put to work. My malaria persisted and I did my work around the hospital while taking quinine treatments."

On 28 January 1942, while being moved from Victoria Barracks to Sham Shuipo prisoner-of-war camp, he found himself in front of what had formerly been the British Military Headquarters known as China Command Building.

"The guards weren't watching me so I decided to take a quick look around. On a table in an alcove I noticed two packets of hard tack, a burned out candle, and a copy of *The New Testament*. On impulse I slipped the book into my pocket. The letters RCS and the numerals 2324023 heavily inked on the outer edges of its pages were the only clues to the former owner."

With fellow prisoners-of-war in Japanese hands, Sergeant Doull was to undergo horrendous hardships for the next four years. He came to know illness, forced marches, inhuman treatment while at North Point and Sham Shuipo, and slave labour while building the Kai Tak Airfield. He was among Canadians transported to Japan on a coal ship in which each prisoner-of-war was allocated one square yard of space in the hold. On that voyage he saw men around him dying of dysentery and dehydration. For the badly undernourished Canadians there followed back-breaking work in the mines and shipyards of Japan. Sergeant Doull contracted beri-beri and dysentery, and his case of trench feet was considered at one point to be terminal.

Although physical and mental endurance were tested to the limit, the soldiers found small ways to ease the strain.

"Early on there was optimistic speculation about a release date and thousands of dollars (to be paid out on return to Canada) were wagered, signed and witnessed, on scraps of toilet paper. It was all very serious at the time but over the years the men were dispersed and the records lost. More immediate payment was frequently made when a man's statement was challenged and a bowl of rice was the forfeit.

"Sometimes we'd put red ants and bed bugs (another scourge of camp life) within a drawn circle and watch the result. Although the ants were smaller, they had ravenous appetites and devoured the bed bugs in short order. It was really no contest."

Eighty-six Canadians died in the winter of 1944 through starvation and harsh physical treatment. At one time mine-sowing Allied aircraft were making twice-nightly raids. The prisoners-of-war, awakened and herded into the hills at each alert, were still required to be ready at 6 a.m. for a hard day's work. Following the bombing of Hiroshima they were to find that their meagre food rations had been further reduced. Even when certain liberation was near their troubles were not over.

"B-29s came over dropping their welcome relief supplies but the big drums, heavy with food, were themselves dangerous. They did a lot of damage to the camp and killed civilians.

Official Nipponese photos were stored with other data, in a

small office of a building which collapsed 7 January 1945 at approximately 0100 hrs killing eight POWs, three of them Canadians. Dispersed through deep snow, the photos were picked up by a Canadian who gave them out to 'matching faces' – secretly. Nipponese search tours to recover documents and photographs were unsuccessful.

Throughout his long internment and all that went with it, the Roman Catholic bible stayed with Protestant Lloyd Doull.

"In dire straits such as we were in, men have often relied on faith and I was no exception. I drew much-needed comfort from the book and its message helped sustain my morale.

"Once the Japanese had stamped the first page, they never bothered to go past that point on their regular inspections. It was easy for me to store small scraps of Red Cross toilet paper among its pages. I made notations on the paper that related to the deaths of our boys."

Sadly that data was not to return to Canada with him as he had planned. One day in August 1945, just prior to the end of hostilities, while the Canadians were away working, their belongings were thoroughly searched. *The New Testament* was emptied of its extra and precious records.

During the post-war years, Lloyd Doull often speculated on the fate of the Testament owner. Had he been killed in battle, died from wartime hardships, or since, or was he alive and available for contact?

In 1974 a letter of enquiry was sent to the Royal British Legion who forwarded it to the Royal Signals Association. No. 2324023 it turned out, was still living.

At the secret invitation of the Lt-Colonel M.E.E. Truscott, Lloyd and Margaret Doull (ex-RCAF (WD)) attended the seventh reunion of survivors of the Royal Corps of Signals Hong Kong Company. At the army base in southern England in August 1975, the rest of the Company were puzzled about the unexplained Canadian presence at their very exclusive celebration.

Following the reunion dinner, Monty Truscott called Lloyd Doull and one of the British chaps forward.

"Is this yours?" asked Lloyd Doull.

"Yes, it's mine," replied William Devlin, thoroughly mystified.

Then Lloyd Doull told all the men, who listened intently, of its finding and his association with it during the long days and nights when privation and death had been constant companions.

William Devlin, asked how he felt at the return of his book, commented, "As Lloyd told how he gained solace from reading it in prison camp, I had this peaceful feeling of elation and realized that my *New Testament* had been on a crusade of its own."

Lloyd Doull, retired safety engineer, still lives in Drummondville, Quebec. He and his wife Margaret have both worked long and steadily to benefit the cause of Canadian veterans who were prisoners of the Japanese.

14

Capturing Pig Swill

Lewis McFawn of Fredericton, New Brunswick was seventeen and unemployed when he decided to join the Royal Rifles of Canada in 1940. Shortly afterwards he was on his way to Hong Kong with the regiment and the next four years of his youth were spent trying to stay alive.

IN 1980 HE WENT back to visit the places where he had existed as a prisoner-of-war in Japanese hands.

"I was fine in Hong Kong but as soon as we landed in Japan the old feeling came back as strong as ever. One of the guys summed up the way I felt when he remarked later – 'We didn't know whether they were going to shake hands or shoot us.' I felt as if I was a POW again, on edge and wary as a cat. I know now that it's there still, for me."

One of McFawn's wartime recollections is concerned with successfully putting one over on his captors. The Japanese were feeding up a pig for their own table – "most certainly not for the mouths of Canadian prisoners!" Anyway, in the desperate long-drawn-out game of survival young McFawn took a chance or two. He'd watch for the Japanese to give the animal its food and then as soon as the guards were out of sight, he'd slip in and snatch most of the swill to share it with his fellow POWs. While telling the tale with retrospective relish he remarked "For sure, it was better than anything WE got. We put on a little fat and the pig put on a little less."

Men who were there know the desperation and risks involved in such audacious behaviour.

Editor's Note: The original strength of the Canadian C Force stood at 1,973. Of this number, 286 were killed in battle; 493 were wounded in action; 129 died of illness while prisoners in Japanese hands.

Lewis McFawn resides in Fredericton, N.B.

15

Casualty Clearing

Lieutenant Nursing Sister **Mary Bray** in battle dress, Belgium 1944.

It had been September 1942 when Mary, a young Montreal nurse who was visiting friends in Pictou, Nova Scotia had the sudden urge "to dash up to Halifax and join the army". Within three weeks she was posted to a transient camp at Debert, N.S. where she worked for sixteen months. Her desired but exhausting journey to the Rhine and beyond, had begun.

WANTING TO GO overseas, Lieutenant N/S M. Bray sailed from Halifax in January 1944 on the small troopship *Cavina*. The 100 vessel convoy arrived in Liverpool eighteen days later.

"For five mornings the ship's doctor and I were the only ones well enough to face breakfast. Our bath steward, whose job was to supply us with a bucket of fresh water to rinse ourselves after a salt water bath, was caught stealing nurses' money belts. And at Liverpool an army officer and a nursing sister announced their engagement."

Exterior and interior views of the Canadian Army Hospital at Camp Debert, Nova Scotia in 1943.

Mary Bray was posted to No. 18 General Hospital at Colchester for two months and billetted in an old mansion, Blenheim House.

"An American doctor who'd married a classmate of mine, was attached to a nearby Thunderbolt fighter squadron. A sneak raider had downed a Lancaster and George salvaged parachute nylon for us; it was highly prized for making underwear. Arranging for some of us to go over to their 'drome, he suggested, 'I'll send an ambulance and you fill it up with nurses.' We liked to go there, particularly for the food. The Americans always had delicacies that we never saw. It was something too, to watch the Thunderbolts take off and return."

Her next posting was to a Canadian Casualty Clearing Station in the Hotel Metropole, Folkestone.

"Noisy wasn't the word for it. As well as the regular cross-Channel shelling there were frequent low-flying buzz bombs sputtering away overhead, and the ack-ack fire crackling around them.

"At each shelling alert we'd shepherd most of the patients down to the basement. Tired or not, we eight nurses had to march up and down the hills of Folkestone with full packs. And we had to tolerate the amused laughter of soldiers."

A few weeks after D Day she was up at 4 a.m. and boarding a truck headed for Southampton. On arrival at the Concentration Area they were told that they would set sail soon after midnight. Under canvas, the nurses snatched some sleep on stretchers, then awoke to find that although their gear had gone aboard ship, there was no provision to transport women. Along with personnel from two other casualty clearing stations, they waited a further two days without a toothbrush or change of anything. Eventually they embarked on a British hospital ship for a choppy Channel crossing and debarked on to a French beach from a landing craft.

"As we left her, we noticed the hospital ship was taking on sailors whose ship had struck a mine. Huge basket things were used to rescue those oil-blackened men from the sea. Ashore we met a truck full of bomb-wacky Canadians headed for the same ship. 'Don't let those girls go up there. It's terrible. Don't go up there,' those poor kids kept yelling at our Matron."

That night, the first Canadian hospital in France was set up under canvas.

"By noon there was no time to think. Just do. We worked like crazy. Surgical teams were already operating and our 'ward' was full of seriously wounded men. Private or Brigadier, they were side by side in cots. Many seemed so very young; from then on it was hard for me to accept what war could do.

"Our fifth day there happened to be my birthday but I didn't give it a thought. An officer friend came round but he was not permitted to see me because I was too busy. He left me a birthday bottle of rye. When we went off duty that night it was pouring rain, water was coming in the tents, and the big guns were flashing and booming to the rear. We were glad of the rye to help us get to sleep.

"All casualties came through the three CCCSs where doctors classified them. We usually attended to all serious abdominal injuries and urgent amputations while other cases were sent back to hospitals in the rear. When possible, patients were built up prior to surgery with plasma and intravenous solutions. All abdominals were given a cholostomy to rest damaged organs, the incision to be closed later. Three or four teams of surgeons operated steadily.

"One young fellow who'd had his butt shot off would say to me, 'Just hate to ask you but would you please change my dressing?' Then he'd repeat this little rhyme. 'By gum chum, my bum's numb.' I met him years later and he was still having trouble."

From a letter published in Canada, N/S Mary Bray was quoted "The best is not too good for them and it breaks our hearts to be so busy that we can't give them more attention." She was so busy that she collided with General Crerar on the ward and it was only when she was introduced to him later that she realized just whom she had almost knocked over.

Moving up with the troops, their next stop was near Carpiquet Airfield, Normandy.

"Our forces had gone up as far as Caen and fighting had been violent. There were a lot of dead bodies lying around and a horrible stench was everywhere. Our medical teams were working sixteen hours on and eight hours off, straight.

125

Minefields in the vicinity of the nurses' tents outside Caen, France in 1944.

Nurses' quarters were the tents that summer.

The Army Nursing Sisters travelled from France to Holland, Belgium and Germany in convoy trucks, even sleeping in them on the roadsides.

"We were issued a silly little billycan of water to wash ourselves and do our laundry. For sure we were not the neatest or the cleanest little nurses you'd ever meet! And we'd learned to improvise. Khaki slings served as bandanas for our hair and bandage scissors hung from lariats around our necks.

"Casualties poured in and surgical staff would send them on to us with instructions attached. On one card 'AND WASH BEHIND THE EARS EVERY HOUR' was added; Toronto's Dr. Bill Mustard's sense of humour.

"A young Canadian and a German boy were brought in together. The German had sniped at the Canadian who'd wounded him in turn. From their stretchers they yelled at one another in their own languages. Still fighting mad.

"When Allied planes bombed our troops in error there was a dreadful price paid. The rush of ambulances brought hundreds of wounded just as in a major battle action."

Mary Bray's unit left the Caen area and halted at Lisieux.

"The town, freed only hours before, was holding a Liberation Parade and we joined in. Only the previous night a German foot patrol had entered Lisieux looking for food and had murdered a family to get it. Captured by townspeople, the Germans were forced to dig their own graves before being shot. That violent scene of ritualistic retribution seemed unreal to me. It was as though I was watching a movie."

Into army trucks again and on to Rouen, the ancient capital of Normandy. When the convoy finally stopped, half the nurses ran one way and the rest the other.

"It was pitch dark and my group squatted in a bed of stinging nettles which made me fidgety and uncomfortable for some time. The others ended up on somebody's lawn and a man sent a dog after them."

The Germans had recently left Rouen with Canadians in pursuit. Casualties were light so after a brief stop, No. 3 CCCS moved on to Montrieul where they took over from an enemy casualty clearing unit.

"The German nurses glared at us and we glared back. I noticed that each of them had her own big jug of wine. Conditions were grim. The enemy didn't have penicillin and patients' wounds had been treated wth a foul-smelling concoction. We even found a couple of leeches on a patient. All wounds were re-dressed. Running low on penicillin ourselves, it was decreed that the drug should be used on Allied patients only. Under the Geneva Convention it wasn't necessary to provide more than our boys were getting from the Germans. When we gave our chaps a shot, the German POWs would grin from ear to ear because they were not getting a needle and our boys were.

"At Montrieul our Matron and our Quartermaster decided to get married. And somehow, in the middle of hostilities, the Colonel found them 'a nice little spot by a lake' for a week's honeymoon."

Always following closely behind the advancing Canadians, Mary Bray and her RCAMC colleagues next stopped at Lokeren, Belgium. In the cold and damp of late fall, tents were hastily pitched and patients received. The nurses bought themselves wooden shoes and preserved their leather ones.

"I developed cystitis and conditions were not the best for recovery. At night we'd get into our cots taking all our clothes with us, then to keep dry we'd bundle ourselves and our clothes inside our rubber groundsheets. When the cystitis pain got bad I'd have to unwrap myself from my cocoon, put on my clomping wooden shoes and get my medicine. And then bundle up again – to the moans and groans of the girls I'd disturbed.

"Our damp tent hospital was eventually exchanged for a school in Niklaas and the nurses were billetted in the local nunnery. I'm sure the nuns were quite shocked at our slacks and short skirts but they were very kind to us."

At Antwerp, the group lived in barracks and among their patients were Dutch civilians injured by bombs or mines.

'We'd found a filthy old bathtub in the barracks and after much scouring and scrubbing, I drew the lot to have the first bath. I was relaxing blissfully in the unusual luxury when a V2 dropped nearby and the whole ceiling fell in. I escaped injury but the tub and I were both dirtier than ever."

Off again, towards Nijmegen, Holland. Columns and columns of Canadian troops marched past their convoy showing obvious delight at the sight of Canadian girls. The medical team relieved a British CCS whose personnel had been isolated for twenty days.

"The Germans were just across the river at Arnhem and we

were shot at almost continually. The army thought that we were too close to the enemy but nevertheless asked for volunteers to stay on. I was scared but said I'd stay. One time when the guns started, I ran into a nearby cemetery and jumped into a newly-dug grave.

"An officer I knew well was brought in lying on his stomach, wounded seriously in the buttocks. I gave him his shot of morphine and he told me later that he didn't wake until after his operation in a British hospital. He'd been a bit annoyed that I could do that to him!".

No. 77 British General Hospital
14 February 1945

Dear Mary,

I am really furious now!! Here I am in an English Base Hospital in Ghent. I don't mind being in Base Hospital and I don't mind being in Ghent, but why can't I be in a Canadian Hospital?

It is funny the things they worry about in the various stages of your trip back. From Regimental Aid Post to Casualty Clearing Station they seemed to worry whether I had 4 blankets or not. From Canadian General Hospital to Base they worried whether I had tops to my pyjamas. At Base they worry about whether you have signed for your towel and slippers. By now I have completely forgotten about being sick and spend my time checking to see whether I have my pants on, and counting my blankets, etc.

I thought you were my friend when you started me on penicillin but now I'm beginning to wonder – as I can't seem to stop them giving it to me. It keeps one occupied thinking up new places to have the next needle.

I was up and walking around today a bit, so I must be nearly better. I have to go back to the operating room tomorrow to get sewn up again. The CGH was pretty good except they woke me up to give me morphine to make me sleep, which didn't seem at all right somehow.

At No. 3 CCS I saw my favourite nurse – definitely the highlight of the whole trip. I think I could have talked her into letting me stay there but didn't as I was 'afeared'. Yes, afeared of falling in love with her. Funny eh! Wish I had taken the chance though now.

John

"We rejoined our unit at Grave and were once again in barracks. I went to a Christmas party given by Canadian Engineers for Dutch children. I could not believe those children. In spite of all their deprivations or perhaps because of them, they would not open their gifts until they got home. They sang us this little song about St. Nicholas and clacked their wooden shoes together. I found it very moving."

GRAVE 5 December 44 We will try in this way to express our well meant thanks to the Allied authorities and soldiers who made it possible that our children had such a happy and pleasant Santerklaus feast, the cordial and kindly entertainment and the many deliciousnesses with which they have been surprised.

We will hope that you will be convinced of the many thanks of their fathers and mothers. (a newspaper excerpt)

"I was invited to a party in an Officers Mess nearly fifty miles away. My escort came to pick me up in a tank and we had to lie down all the way. My husband loves that story!

"Back to Nijmegen and billetted in another school, we were not allowed out over the holiday period because the Germans were threatening to drop parachutists.

"Our troops were being rested and rotated, and I was among nurses given a short holiday. We flew to England in an unheated Lancaster that happened to be piloted by a son of friends of my parents. A fellow passenger was a brigadier who asked our help in getting some grouse into England. At

Canada House, where they claimed no knowledge of us and could not find us accommodation, our brigadier came to the rescue. He went straight to the top. 'I've four young Canadian women here who've not had a proper bath in months. All they need is a warm bath and a comfortable bed' he told Vincent Massey, the High Commissioner. That worked. The first night we stayed in a hostel but from then on in a high class Knightsbridge hotel where everyone dressed for dinner. The amount of cutlery had us guessing but what the heck, there was a war on and we made the most of our leave.

"The Lancaster pilot rounded up some chaps for an evening out. When the airmen wanted to buy us something we suggested a replacement for our Lili Marlene record which had been played and played in Holland until it got broken. They thought it a peculiar request but came through. Actually, they stole it from a pub that same night."

On the nurses' return their unit had moved into a picturesque moated castle at Lochem, Holland. There was no going into town at first because a German sniper was lodged inside a turret on the city hall and shot at people for three days. A German reconnaissance vehicle drove up to the castle, found to their surprise that it was a Canadian hospital, and drove off again without incident.

"After completing a bridge, a group of our Engineers had been rewarded with Calvados which turned out to be bad. Although they were treated promptly the tragedy was that some of them were permanently blinded. Patients at that stage included a number of refugees walking back home from Germany on raw and bleeding feet.

"We moved on and found ourselves ahead of the troops. They'd moved back into the forest area to prepare for the crossing of the Rhine. Shells were zooming over us a lot of the time. Mathew Halton, the Canadian war correspondent visited but we had no time to talk to him at length. He mentioned on his radio programme that while he was at the hospital there was a loud explosion and Nursing Sister Mary Bray had remarked 'That was a close one' and gone on with her work. What had he expected me to do?

"We were amazed when German civilians at that location

The Canadian 'Castle' hospital at Lochem, Holland.

lined up to bow us in and out of the john. At Easter in 1945 our fervent prayers were for an early and successful crossing of the Rhine."

During the wait, nurses were sent by pairs to Paris for forty-eight hour leaves. Mary Bray went with a girl who was not a regular with the unit and barely known to her. On arrival in Paris Lieut. N/S Bray contacted an acquaintance who was the Canadian Army Education Officer.

"He arranged for us to be shown the city and that evening we were taken to the Folies Bérgère and another top night spot. Escorted by two officers, we ended up at an Officers Club for dancing. By then my nurse friend was quite inebriated. 'Mary,

Patients and staff at Lochem, early in 1945.

come and see what I can do' she begged me. I followed her out on to the balcony where she demonstrated how she'd been jumping down into the arms of a gendarme standing below! I knew that she was beyond listening to my advice so I went back to dancing. Then someone decided that my partner and I were not dancing close enough and banged us together. His chin hit me squarely in the eye! Back in our room later, I waited for the other nurse but she never turned up. Next morning one of the chaps phoned saying that she'd been running about the hotel all night and would I please go and collect her. We finally arrived back with our unit one day late and me with the shiner! My friend was sent back to a General Hospital; I wasn't even reprimanded."

In March 1945 the Allied armies crossed the Rhine as Hitler's Western Front was collapsing.

"Our Engineers had built impressive bridges but the devastation we saw on both sides of the Rhine was terrrible. We moved up through Germany, often setting up our tent hospital in a field for a short time before pulling out again. We knew that the end of the war must be near. Most German troops coming to us in those closing weeks were not more than fifteen or sixteen years old."

At the end of hostilities Lieutenant Nursing Sister M. Bray sailed back to Canada on the *Ile de France*. Her bomber pilot brother had also served in Europe and arrived home in St. Lambert shortly after Mary.

"I'd often wondered if Jack was up there when the Lancasters roared overhead. On the same day that I received notice of being Mentioned In Dispatches, he heard that he'd been awarded a Distinguished Flying Cross.

"My trunk had finally caught up with me. In it I'd packed a German dagger, some Benedictine and Triple Sec, along with a few other souvenirs. The dagger had somehow embedded itself in the bottle of Triple Sec and my stuff was a horrible mess of things stuck together. The Benedictine was intact so Jack and I celebrated with that."

In 1946 **Mary Bray** married a former officer of the Royal Canadian Navy and settled down to raise a family. She lives with her husband, Mr. D. F. Hutton, in the Toronto area.

16

Headaches for a Fusilier Mont-Royal

Sergeant **Roland Côté**, Les Fusiliers Mont-Royal, and Corporal Joan Skilton, Women's Auxiliary Air Force, were married in the ancient Church of St. Lawrence, Telscombe Village, Sussex, England on 18 July 1942.

A French-Canadian unit, the Régiment de Maisonneuve of Montreal was the first in Canada to fill its ranks with volunteers for overseas service, and General L-R. Lafleche, the deputy-minister of national defence, estimated that 50,000 French Canadians were in uniform by 1 January 1941.
The French Canadians 1760-1945, Mason Wade

IN SPITE OF the ongoing controversy in Quebec regarding the war, young French Canadians were volunteering steadily. The Maisonneuves served in Canada's 2nd Infantry Division as did the Fusiliers Mont-Royal. Young Roland Côté was one such French-Canadian.

"It was the fall of the year 1930, when I was living in Longueil, across the St. Lawrence River. One evening I went to the armory in Montreal on Pine Avenue to enrol in the Fusiliers Mont-Royal, a militia unit. I was eighteen years old.

"Many times I walked from Longueil across the Jacques Cartier Bridge to the armory and back home again; a twenty-mile return trip. Now I was in uniform and I loved the army, to drill with a rifle, marching, and learning how to handle the Lewis gun. After the evening was over we were given a plate of pork and beans and a little package of cigarettes.

"In 1932, I met my very good friend Louis Georges Hogue (Warrant Officer L. G. Hogue killed at Dieppe). In 1934, I was promoted to sergeant. When war was declared in September 1939, we all signed up as privates but after a short while I had my sergeant's stripes back.

"At the end of June 1940, we left Halifax and landed in Iceland. The regiment left to go forty miles inland. I was left behind with fifteen men as a rear party and had at my disposal two three-ton British Army lorries. On the way to my Company I was in the first truck and there were four men and driver in the second one. My driver came to a short sharp curve and missed it, drove in the field to come back on the road but the truck rolled over twice. I was pinned with half my body out of the cab window. I landed on my back and the roof of the cab landed on my stomach. I thanked God that I had my gas mask and pouches in front of me but I couldn't move at all. Some of my men were injured in the back of the truck. The second truck stopped and the four men and driver came running. Those five men, with sheer nerve, lifted the truck back on its wheels. I took the men as quickly as possible to our medical officer.

"After four months in Iceland we left for England. In the fall of 1941 our Company (A Company) was stationed in Telscombe Cliffs on the South Coast. One Saturday evening we held a dance in the Club at Telscombe Village. Suddenly I saw this beautiful girl in WAAF uniform. I went over to her and

135

said 'May I have this dance please?' We looked at each other and we both knew then that we were meant for each other.

"Her name was Joan Skilton and she was stationed at Harrogate in Yorkshire. We hardly saw one another except when we both had leave. In April 1942, we decided to get married. I went to see my colonel (Colonel Dollard Menard) for his permission. His reply was 'Sorry Sergeant, you can't get married yet' and he told me why. 'We are going on special training on the Isle of Wight for three months.'

"At the beginning of July we were put on boats at Newhaven. Then they told us that we were going to make a raid on Dieppe, France. Now we saw why all the special training was given. The weather wasn't in our favour. The last day to make the raid in the morning was on 8 July which was my birthday. On the evening of 7 July the operation was postponed. Each regiment went back to the place where they were stationed.

"Then we all went on leave and my colonel gave me permission to get married. I asked my best friend, Louis Georges Hogue, to be my best man. On 18 July my darling Joan and I were married in the very old Church of St. Lawrence in Telscombe Village where we met. What a beautiful wedding we had.

"Just one month after our wedding, on 18 August Colonel Menard gave orders for everyone to pack personal belongings in kit bags, and get ready for combat. The raid on Dieppe was on again. We left that evening from Shoreham to cross the Channel during the night. We all know how we were received at Dieppe. It was a massacre.

"As we were approaching Dieppe it was still dark. When I saw tracer bullets going and coming on the left towards the commandos, I realized that the element of surprise was gone and we were really in for it. Les Fusiliers Mont-Royal were the floating reserve and we were going in last.

"On the way in to land I saw a couple of my friends shot dead. The feeling that you have in the middle of battle and killing is indescribable but yet you can never ever forget it. Then one of my men was shot in the left arm, piercing the artery. I went to his help and as I pulled him down into the bottom of the landing craft, he fell on top of me. While I was making a

Dieppe with its memorial to the Canadians and with its prominent chateau.

tourniquet to stop the bleeding a shell fell nearby. I remember it spinning us around and then we both went unconscious. When the tide changed our craft floated out into the Channel and we were picked up by a small boat and taken to a destroyer. We landed at Portsmouth and I was first taken to a hospital there and then the Canadian Hospital at Horsham for a few weeks. I suffered a concussion and the very bad headaches lasted about twelve years.

"After my release I was sent to a holding unit and when I rejoined my regiment later, I found that there were only about a hundred men left. We had to start all over again with new men sent from Canada. Our new colonel gave me a promotion, Warrant Officer II confirmed in my rank.

"Early in 1943, Joan received her discharge from the WAAF for she was pregnant. On 22 September she presented me with our son, Roland. Before the invasion in June 1944, every man had to pass a medical. I was re-boarded to be sent back to Canada. I arrived back in Canada at the beginning of May and was sent to be attached to Le Regiment de Joliette as an instructor.

"In October 1944, my war bride arrived in Montreal with our one-year-old son. How happy we were to see one another.

"I was discharged from the army on 3 May 1946. From the beginning of the war I had prayed to God every day asking for health, strength, and courage to carry out my duties as a soldier."

Editor's Note: Dieppe Headaches For A Fusilier Mont-Royal was based on Roland Côté's personal account which he wrote for the records of the Dieppe Veterans and POW Association.

Prior to his retirement in 1972, ex-Sergeant-major **R. Côté,** was employed by the T. Eaton Company. With his wife Joan, he lives in the Montreal area.

17

Take Your Rosary, Son

Sapper **Albert Brown** in his white undershirt marched along with other Canadian prisoners-of-war through the streets of Dieppe on 19 August 1942. The jackboots of the German officer who had just kicked him are visible to his right. In the Summer of 1939, he had been out of school for a year and no matter how hard he had tried, Albert Brown of Sarnia had been unable to find work. So on 7 September 1939 he volunteered for the Canadian army and his employment problem was solved.

On 19 AUGUST 1942 FOLLOWING defence of Britain duty and special training, he would take part, along with nearly 5000 other Canadians, in the short but still contraversial raid on the French port of Dieppe. Just twenty-one, he was with the 11th Field Company, Royal Canadian Engineers.

"My father was a devout Catholic and when I was about to go overseas, he said that if I ever went into action I should be sure to take my rosary with me for protection.

"When our landing craft was lowered into the water and as we headed for the French coast – I most certainly had my rosary with me. In fact, I think I must have set a record for the most Hail Marys in the shortest time! All hell had broken loose even before our landing craft touched shore."

Sapper A. Brown was one of a seven man team of RCES scheduled to demolish a specific concrete roadblock in Dieppe. While sustained enemy fire screamed and burst around him, he made his way over the pebbly beach cautiously carrying sixty pounds of explosives.

"The odds were against me but the worst I got was having the heel of one of my boots shot clean off. My foot wasn't touched."

Five of the demolition team somehow made their way up the beach, across the promenade, and got close to their objective. Few other attackers were able to penetrate into the town. However, the officer in charge and a sixth Sapper of the group had both been seriously wounded on the beach. Without the Sapper, who had carried the fuses and detenators, it was impossible to complete the mission.

For awhile the men took shelter in the Municipal Theatre while shell fire rained down from the old castle on higher ground to the right. The ancient fortress, well defended by a modern German army was located on a prime vantage point. From there Canadians were fired upon early in the day and again later, as they attempted to withdraw.

"Then from the rear of the theatre came the unexpected. One of our tanks began firing into the building. Another fellow and I ran up a flight of stairs to a window. I tore off my battledress tunic and we waved it from the end of a broomstick. This was to get the tank driver's attention and let them know that Canadians, not Germans, were occupying the thea-

The Germans dropped leaflets in England to demoralize the troops with such scenes of captured and dead soldiers on the Dieppe beaches.

tre. The tunic slipped off the end of the broomstick and fell into the street and in the confusion and urgency of the moment, it was lost."

Almost simultaneously German soldiers had burst into the theatre from the front. Three of the five RCEs and several infantrymen made it out of another door. Sappers Albert Brown and Barney Murray were captured. Albert Brown was to spend two years and nine months as a prisoner-of-war.

At the end of war Brown would recognize himself, minus his tunic of course, in a German photograph showing a column of captured Canadains being marched through the streets of Dieppe.

"I had just felt the boot of a German officer in my rear as he barked a command at me to put my hands on my head."

Less than two months after the Dieppe raid the Canadians had their hands tied securely behind their backs: the infamous shackles.

"What a gloomy apprehensive feeling when we were lined up that first morning. For all we knew it could have been the prelude to execution.

"From 7 a.m. until 7 p.m. our hands were tied together in front by rope. After four months there followed a period of nine months when the ropes were replaced by handcuffs and chains. We discovered that the handcuffs could be opened by keys from bully beef cans. In that first winter an escape tunnel was begun under the supervision of the Royal Canadian Engineers. It was completed in the spring and a number of men escaped.

"In that time period I was among a group of fifty POWs sent to work outside the main camp at Lamsdorf. I spent about eight months as one of a work party at a cabinet-making shop in the small town of Oberglogau. Others worked in a sugar factory there.

"One of them was Perry Ross, 2nd Field Coy. RCE, from Toronto. He was working a twelve-hour night shift when a German army officer arrived and asked if he might talk to the Canadians in English. Given permission by the shift foreman, he was conversing his way around the building when he encountered Perry Ross. It turned out that the German had lived in Toronto prior to the war and played in the same

The memorial to the Royal Canadian Engineers who died during the raid on Dieppe was unveiled at Newhaven, Sussex in August 1977.

orchestra as Perry.

"The officer was in charge of a civilian internee camp but was then taking his leave in his hometown, Oberglogau. He invited Perry to spend an evening at his home. The camp commander gave permission and for our part, we all approved — hoping that Perry would benefit from a good meal cooked by the officer's Scottish born wife. The German took responsibility for Perry's return and during the evening asked whether there was anything he could do to make life a little easier. Musician Ross requested an accordian with which to entertain the boys.

"Soon, a good quality accordian and some sheet music arrived for Perry, and several mouth organs for prisoners who could play.

"Back to Lamsdorf again and then thirty-five of us were sent out to a small camp close to a village on the Czechoslovakian border. From there we were marched four or five miles into the forest each morning to work as lumberjacks. We cut timber for mine props. Hard work but food rations were slightly better than at Lamsdorf and it was healthier for us to be occupied than sitting around nursing the 'Poor Me's'."

Russian forces were pushing westward and early in 1945, the POWs at Lamsdorf could hear distant artillery.

Herded together by their German guards, the Canadians began several hundred miles and five months of forced marches. Ahead of the advancing Russians they marched and rested, marched and rested, in the pattern of the Soviet troops. It was obvious that the Germans were extremely fearful of encountering the Russians. By 7 May the German guards had disappeared and the first Russian army men were seen.

"A group of us decided to make our own way west to meet American or British forces. We helped ourselves to an abandoned German army truck and provisions. Off we went down the Autobahn but we were soon stopped by Russians and we surrendered the truck. Next we took a team of German army horses and a waggon but we were soon stopped by Russians again and they took our transport. A couple of days later we joined some French army officers (POWs) and took control of a railway locomotive and a string of boxcars. About 2000 of us, POWs and displaced persons from God knows where, all clambering on that train. But fifteen to twenty miles down the line it happened again. The Russians commandeered the engine. A week later and we'd persuaded them to let us have a replacement and so we reached Pilsen, Czechoslovakia and the Americans!

"Next day we were flown to Brussels and the following one to England. There followed three weeks of hospital convalescence, some leave, and then it was home to Canada."

In November 1974, Rose Eykel of St. Lambert near Montreal, was in Paris, France. She decided to walk from her hotel to the nearest beauty salon. While an assistant worked on Mrs. Eykel's hair, the owner, Madame Angéle Pointereau, was tidying up prior to leaving for Dieppe where she spent her weekends.

"Angéle, hearing that I was a Canadian, began telling me the story behind some articles long in her possession. At the time of the Dieppe raid she had been living in an apartment above the Municipal Theatre and with her mother, she had been watching at the window as a soldier's tunic fell from the second floor to the street below."

When the fighting ceased, the women recovered the Canadian army tunic, removed the contents from its pockets and returned the jacket to the street for the Germans to find. The few personal belongings of the Canadian soldier were boxed and buried in a garden adjoining the theatre. Angéle dug them up at the end of the war and took them to Paris.

"She brought out the items that she had preserved carefully and asked me to trace the owner and return them to him or his family. With the help of the Legion and the Canadian Army, I was happy to do this on my return to Montreal."

And so it was that on 15 December 1974 Albert Brown, employed at Polysar, Sarnia for twenty-nine years, heard that his long-given-up-for-lost possessions were about to be returned to him.

When they arrived, none the worse for their adventure, he looked at the objects in amazement. Once again there was the rosary in its leather pouch; the rosary that he had bought in Ireland in 1940, and carried into the ill fated battleground of Dieppe. There was the leather folder with his crucifix, religious medals, and identity card (the latter made it easier to trace him). A little wartime book of British stamps and his photographs completed his 1942 army jacket's contents.

"It was truly astonishing to see the things again so unexpectedly after thirty-two years."

Al Brown had been back to Dieppe in August 1972, and in March 1974. Now he was in touch with Angéle Pointereau hoping to return again, to meet her.

He had never forgotten his Royal Canadian Engineer comrades. He had seen memorials in Dieppe to the dead of other units and felt that the Engineers should have a permanent monument. He undertook to form a committee for the purpose.

"On 17 August 1977, the memorial was unveiled at Newhaven, England. So many of us trained in and around there. Some who took part in the Dieppe raid set out from Newhaven, and many returned to the port."

The next day he crossed the English Channel again and appropriately on 19 August, he kept a rendezvous with Angéle Pointereau and her husband, Maurice. While Marc Pilote, (a Dieppe veteran of the Fusiliers Mont-Royal), acted as interpreter, they talked of 19 August 1942, and how their paths had crossed that day.

To the man from Sarnia, the Municipal Theatre looked much the same as in 1942. He remembered the incident clearly: two young soldiers at a second floor window anxiously waving a khaki Canadian army tunic draped on the end of a broomstick.... the tunic falls into the Dieppe street below.... from a window on the third floor, a young French woman takes note of its descent.... For Albert Brown the circle was complete.

Albert Brown with his rescued rosary.

Albert Brown kindly related his story to the author and sent his 'lost and found' treasures for her to see, prior to his death in 1980.

18

No Nervous Breakdowns

Of course we were under immense pressure at times but none of the Nursing Sisters I knew had nervous breakdowns. We were too busy to think of ourselves.

We knew so many lads who'd be going off to the front line the next day; some never returned and some would come back to us as casualties."

Captain (Matron) **Margaret Kellough** had grown up in Almonte in the Ottawa Valley. In spite of family opposition to the idea for they thought it an extremely arduous profession, she clung to her dream of becoming a nurse. As a naive eighteen-year-old she had applied to train at the Toronto General Hospital. There, she had gained the experience and skills which would prove invaluable as WWII and her own career developed.

O<small>N</small> 8 <small>SEPTEMBER</small> 1939, I wrote to the Red Cross. On 9 September, I went and signed up. And on 10 September I was sworn in as an Army Nursing Sister."

September 10 just happened to be the day that Canada declared war on Germany. Later when she received her new Royal Canadian Army Medical Corps nurse's uniform, Lieutenant (Nursing Sister) Margaret Kellough began work at the old Grace Hospital on Collgee Street near Spadina Avenue, Toronto.

"We treated soldiers quartered at the Horse Palace in the Canadian National Exhibition grounds. Some were accident cases but a good many suffered chest infections caused by the incessant dust from the concrete floors in their makeshift barracks."

The Unit was designated for overseas duty and on 7 June 1940, she was one of 80 Army nurses who travelled from Toronto along with 50 from Winnipeg to board a troopship at Halifax. The crossing on the *Duchess of Bedford* was hazardous with numerous U boat and mine alerts, and although escorted in convoy, the ship's Captain never left the bridge.

France capitulated while the *Duchess of Bedford* was crossing the Atlantic and so her destination had to be changed from Dieppe to Liverpool. Margaret Kellough joined the Canadian staff of a Nissen hut hospital on the Portsmouth road, at Bramshott in Hampshire, England. Canadian service personnel were treated there for illnesses and for injuries caused by motor-cycle accidents and sundry other mishaps. After the Dieppe Raid, August 1942, the more seriously wounded of the returning Canadians were taken to the hospital.

By June 1943, Lt. (Assistant-Matron) Margaret Kellough was boarding another ship, destination unknown. Once at sea, the Nursing Sisters began taking mepracrine, an antidote for malaria. They were issued new khaki uniforms, high laced boots and leather gaiters. Their destination was revealed to be El Arrouch, Algeria, North Africa.

On 13 May 1943, General Alexander had signalled Winston Churchill thus: *Sir: It is my duty to report that the Tunisian campaign is over. All enemy resistance has ceased. We are masters of the North African shores.*

Nursing Sisters and their bicycles lined up at Bramshott, England near No.15 Canadian General Hospital, RCAMC.

Following the cessation of hostilities any newly-arriving staff became ineligible for the North Africa Star. However, the Canadian hospital at El Arrouch went on caring for Canadian and British sick and wounded.

"We worked in a tented hospital where the lighting system consisted of hurricane lanterns and flashlights. Only the Operating Room had electricity. And there were flies, fleas, filth and locals to contend with!

"It was so hot that as soon as siesta began we'd strip off our uniforms, wash and hang out the khaki shirts and skirts and they'd be dry for our return to duty. Having no irons, we folded our skirts in three and put them between newspaper under our cot mattresses. It was surprising how well they looked. We'd even go to dances in those outfits. After sundown in malaria season we had to wear slacks, boots and gaiters. Shirt sleeves were kept rolled down and faces were covered in anti-mosquito cream. What an alluring group we must have been!

"We slept under mosquito nets. And the nets were pulled

down over all patient's beds at sundown, to be raised only at sunup, somewhat hampering our care of the patients."

Creatures such as chameleons, lizards, centipedes and locusts abounded. Voracious appetites of locusts left great holes in the nurse's silk underwear as it hung out to dry. The insects also developed an avid taste for the Medical Officers' peaked caps. The nurses' compound was under guard but armed soldiers were no deterrent to these indigenous attackers.

" 'Suck out the poison immediately if you're bitten' we were warned. During one siesta, stripped down to bra and panties and sitting with one leg crossed over the other, I was dreamily watching perspiration dripping from my dangling heel when suddenly I felt a sharp jab in my seat. I shot up and saw that the culprit had been a large centipede. Not being a contortionist and hardly able to ask a friend to suck out the poison, I decided to trust to luck and my good health, and I toughed it out.

"Occasionally we'd go to the local market. It was an exotic and colourful place but so smelly – mostly from the slaughter of goats. We were escorted by one or more officers for we were never allowed out alone.

"Dr. Bill Oille from Toronto did research connected with malaria and Arab children. He'd obtain the necessary permission and then set out in a jeep with driver, interpreter, and a different Nursing Sister each time. We had to be extremely careful with our antiseptic procedures. Usually we went to the local boys' school where the teacher might be a thirteen-year-old able to recite the Koran extremely well. Girls received no education.

"French fruitgrowers permitted us to pick oranges, the first we'd eaten since leaving Canada. Several of us contracted diarrhoea from either too much fruit, or from the ever-present flies around it.

"On one occasion in North Africa the strong hot winds, a sirocco, broke down tent poles and we nurses and orderlies pitched in to move patients out. And there was the night of the total lunar eclipse. It was awesome and eerie. Particularly so because we'd had no prior knowledge of it."

While the unit personnel awaited transportation to the Italian theatre of war they had begun admitting casualties

The 1200 bed-tented Canadian General Hospital at El Arrouch, Algeria, North Africa.

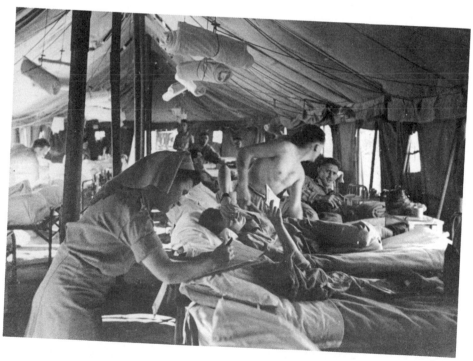

Inside a crowded hospital tent ward in El Arrouch, Algeria.

from the action in Sicily. Margaret Kellough would be awarded the ARRC (Associate Royal Red Cross) for her work in North Africa.

Early in 1944, she was in Caeserta, Italy and living in barracks originally built for Mussolini's troops.

"Vesuvius was only seventeen miles away and erupted once while we were there. Its glow lit up the whole sky and molten ash was carried as far as Caeserta."

She would now use all her skill and experience to alleviate the suffering of wounded soldiers as they arrived from the bitter fighting along the Hitler and Gothic Lines.

"With only field dressings on their wounds, some 200 men a day were arriving straight from the battle area. To accommodate them we had to keep moving out a corresponding number of convalescents. We were equipped as a 1200 bed hospital yet somehow coped with 1700 patients. Operating staff worked straight eight hours on and eight hours off."

From Caeserta she went to No. 5 Canadian Casualty Clearing Station adjacent to the front. A scant six or seven miles (10 to 11 km) from the German lines, No. 5 alternated with CCCS No. 4 in moving forward with the troops, leap-frog fashion. Limited facilities and personnel decreed that their patients were only the most seriously and dangerously wounded men.

"We'd just take over schools, hotels or houses. Most were damaged, some rooms without roofs, but it was effort that counted and everyone worked hard and efficiently. It was literally a matter of life and death. Being a small unit and needing to move quickly at short notice, we carried a minimum of equipment. Wires would be strung along walls of rooms and these held bottles of blood and plasma and other vital medical supplies. Wounded men were brought in and assessed. Operations would be performed immediately while they lay on stretchers. Time was crucial.

"In Ravenna thick dust rolled into the improvised operating room when a bomb fell outside an open window. Surgeons covered the patient's incision, carried the stretcher to another room and continued the operation. That bomb was a dud otherwise we'd all have had it. We were treating wounded from several Allied countries plus some German prisoners of war. Among the latter were boys of fifteen and a few of them were regular little Hitlers.

"One of our most extraordinary patients was a certain Major Peniakoff, a Belgian of Russian parentage and leader of a small reconnaisance and raiding force. They lived in their Jeeps and made dead of night sorties to wipe out enemy gun sites and thereby assist the Allied advance. General Montgomery had difficulty remembering the name Peniakoff and he decided to call him Popski. From then on it was Popski and his Private Army. Major Peniakoff's wounds included an almost completely severed hand which had to be amputated, bullet wounds in his other hand and in one of his ears."

Margaret Kellough's nursing duties next took her to North-West Europe. At Oss, Holland in March 1945, she and a Red Cross worker were billetted with the de Bourbon family. Charles Henri de Bourbon was the mayor of Oss and a member of the Dutch underground. Told by Madame de Bourbon that she looked Dutch, the Canadian girl was persuaded to wear a national costume and pose for a photograph in their garden. She kept in touch with them for a while after the war but then lost contact. In 1975 she read in *The Globe and Mail* that Prince Louis Jean Henri Charles de Bourbon had died at The Hague and that his three children lived in Canada. Meeting the young de Bourbons again, she showed them the photo, and another of Canadian Nursing Sisters in an Easter 1945 march-past. The saluting base was in front of the Town Hall and three little faces were peering from the window of their father's office.

"In April 1945, most of our Medical Officers and N/Ss had been sent to help at Arnhem. One night, under cover of thick fog, Germans got across the canal and headed towards Oss. We were hastily picked up from our billets and taken by truck to the hospital where we spent two nights. Fortunately, the Germans were repulsed before reaching town.

"We moved up through Arnhem to Harskamp. By that time I'd applied for compassionate leave because my mother was seriously ill. When my replacement arrived I was flown to England to await a ship for Canada — and just in time to celebrate VE Day in London.

"Victory in Europe was history but we were still at war with Japan and ships were sailing under black-out regulations. On the stormy crossing of the Brittanica in late May 1945, the passengers included 150 wives of Canadian servicemen and their 350 children. I was in charge of all female personnel on board.

"The war brides had the cabins while our staff of seventeen were assigned to hold where we couldn't even open a porthole for air. Mothers were often called over the intercom because they'd left their children unattended in upper bunks, and in various corners of the ship toddlers were vomiting after being over-indulged with candy.

"Of course there were wiser heads among the women. I felt great sympathy for a young Scottish mother whose infant child died of a thymus condition during the voyage. Very early one morning we held a short service and buried the baby at sea. I had no appetite for breakfast that day."

Editor's Note: When war ended the nursing services of Canada had recruited 4480 nursing sisters and their professional associates. Army: 3656, RCN: 343, RCAF: 481. Canadian nursing sisters in three services won 386 awards of the Royal Red Cross.... More than 100 were mentioned in dispatches. *Canada's Nursing Sisters* by Gerald Nicholson.

Captain (Matron) **M. Kellough** ARRC was discharged from the Army in May, 1946 and continued her contribution to Canada by a lifetime career dedicated to the nursing profession. Now retired, she resides in Toronto.

19

It Could Always Be Worse

Leslie Conrad, born Leslaw Konrad-Korzeniowski in Opaka, Poland served as an artillery officer in the Western Desert and Italy with the 2nd Polish Corps. Those combat experiences had been preceded by a series of even more harrowing events. Leslaw was photographed as a cadet at the Reserve Officer's School, Lwow, Poland, 18 July 1939.

I HAD JUST COMPLETED my education in law when, being a reserve officer, I was mobilized into the Polish Army. I have never had the chance to practice law.

"In September 1939, after a skirmish at Tarnapol, the Russians disarmed us. I changed into civilian clothes, escaped and walked back to my home in Lwow; this escape may well have been an important key to my survival. A month later my fiancee, Maria Voelpel, and I were married.

"It was close to 3 a.m. on 29 February 1940, when Russian soldiers came for me. 'Don't bring anything' they said. 'It's just a check and you'll be home again tomorrow.' They were really looking for a distant cousin of Mary's who was an underground organizer and an ex-Polish Army officer. I was not a member of the group but each night I was interrogated and urged to admit that I did belong, and to give names. Otherwise they said, my wife would be tortured. I was forced to write a dictated card instructing Mary to tell everything she knew – or I should be tortured. Normally I called her Marisia but the Russian fellow dictated Marushka so I wrote it their way and by that Mary knew that I was writing under their orders. Until I was taken away to the labour camp, she was subjected several times to questioning and scare tactics. There was no real evidence against me and I was about to be released when a young man broke under torture and told them that I knew of the underground movement, which I did and had not admitted. For that I was tried and sentenced to ten years hard labour. Subsequent events would mean that my wife and I would be separated for twenty years.

"With others from Lwow, I was put on a train of cattle wagons. No water to drink and salted herring to eat. When I read Solzhenitsyn's book I thought that some of his experiences could have been my own, exactly. They fed us so little and we soon became too weak for any sort of resistance. At some stops they would make us kneel down and stay that way. And guards would shout at us, 'One step forward, one step back, one step left, one step right. I shall shoot without warning.' In any case you were too stiff and weak to try to escape.

"We arrived at Arkangelesk in May. Trucks transported us to a place whose name I can't remember but we walked thirty miles from there to Malaszujka labour camp near Lake Onega.

They handed us axes and said, 'That is your place, build your-selves living quarters' and this we did, using logs and rough wood for the walls and canvas for the top. It housed about a hundred men.

"There were trees all around but under threat of punish-ment, we were forbidden to bring in any wood except that allocated for the central stove, the only heating for our tent-hut barrack. We worked seven days a week constructing rail-way lines and when the work was under five kilometres away, we walked both ways. In wintertime with ten hours of hard physical work, it would add up to twelve hours out there in the snow and bitter cold every day. Sanitary conditions were almost non-existent; lavatories were trenches with logs across. We made a game of counting the number of times you had to leave the barrack to relieve yourself. One night I fell down and passed out and would surely have frozen to death outside had not someone pulled me back into the tent. Crawling with lice, we held competitions each night, to see who could kill the most.

"I'd estimate that there were about 2000 men in the camp and seventy per cent were Poles. We had quite a lot of well-to-do Jews who'd been forced at gun-point by the Germans to cross into Russian-held territory. They were unaccustomed to hard conditions and were dying like flies. Through my army training I had been fit and it helped me survive. But many died, not only the Jews.

"A couple of times they brought women to a special barrack that was surrounded by barbed wire. They were mostly Rus-sian dissenters and thieves; as with the men there was no separation of political prisoners and common criminals. Most of the Russians running the camp were criminals serving their sentences.

"During that winter, and particularly around the time the Jews arrived, corpses would be piled up near the latrine, naked and frozen. Every time you went there you had to pass them. A grim and appalling sight I can't forget. There was a once-a-week dig to bury the bodies and I was on the digging brigade only once. It was very hard to get below the solidly frozen top layer of ground. We only had picks and shovels and it took us three-quarters of the day to get through it. Below that, the digging was easier.

"I had only one day off work in the fifteen months at the camp. That was New Year's Day 1941 when they took us all outside for an official count. My name came before the middle of the alphabet so I was one of the luckier ones. At around -30 degrees some men stood out there until mid-afternoon.

"At one point a Red Cross delegation was expected. There was a big clean-up and we were warned to say that everything was satisfactory. Usually we had to make do with only our clothes but we were issued with blankets – and the night after the Red Cross people left, they took them away again. We'd also had much better food before and during the five days or so of their visit.

"A lot of men picked over the refuse. One elderly professor was always first at the throw-outs. How could you tell a starving old man that he shouldn't do it?

"There was hardly any salt and sugar at all, once we were given 200 grams of marmalade as a sugar substitute: only once. While I was in that camp my dream was to be able to eat and eat until I could eat no more. Just bread would have done, even the soggy black bread we were barely existing on. Parcels were sent to us from Poland but very few reached us. 'Sign' they told us and when we protested that we'd had no parcel, they'd say 'You can write to Moscow about it and we'll keep you here until we find the guilty persons.' I believe the people in charge took our parcels.

"Also when you were about to be released you were asked to sign that your belongings were intact. Belongings that had long since disappeared. If you objected it was 'Alright, you stay until we solve the matter.' Who wanted to stay?".

On July 30, after many bitter discussions, agreement was reached between the Polish and Russian Governments. Diplomatic relations were restored, and a Polish army was to be formed on Russian soil and subordinated to the supreme command of the Soviet Government....

and during the autumn the Poles were occupied in the grim task of collecting their nationals who had survived captivity in the prison camps of the Soviet Union. *The Second World War, Volume III, The Grand Alliance,* Winston S. Churchill.

There had been inklings in the Malaszujka camp that some major change was to happen.

"We were working on a railway line going to Murmansk and passengers would occasionally drop newspapers to us and we'd read that an agreement was likely in regard to a Polish force in Russia.

"Amnesty was granted and we were released in small groups but with no specific information regarding the whereabouts of the Polish army. My release came on 21 August 1941. Because we'd heard that a lot of Poles were in Kazakhstan, three of us headed for southern Russia on the other side of the Ural Mountains. A spectacular sunrise, seen from the train as we journeyed through the Urals, was so beautiful. Everyone gathered and admired.

We stopped at Kustanay where we were read a letter supposed to be from the Polish army advising us not to go to join, that the army was full. We should stay on at the state collective farm and work for the good of Russia and her allies. I recall a poster there; it carried a slogan which roughly translated meant Each Shovel of Earth Dug Out Is a Blow On Hitler's Back.

"Wanting no part of that, my two friends and I jumped on the next train without money or tickets. We told some Russian soldiers aboard that we were trying to find the Polish army and they hid us when the conductor came round. At Saratov we learned that the army headquarters was in Kuybyshev, not far away. And so I became an active Polish soldier again, for the time being training on Russian soil.

"General Anders, our commander, who had been held and mistreated himself, was very much against being under Russian command and we were sure that if necessary, he would fight his way out of the Soviet Union. Fortunately, an agreement was reached whereby our force would join the British forces stationed in the Middle East. We left Russia without hindrance.

After being freed from Russian camps to form their own fighting forces, the Poles arrived in Iran and Lieutenant Conrad posed atop the sign post.

Lieutenant Conrad is on the left in front of Barclay's Bank.

"It took four or five days to cross the Caspian Sea. We were literally packed like sardines on that Russian ship. When we landed there in April 1942, Iran (then Persia) seemed like heaven. The British troops gave us a warm welcome, tents, supplies and food. Food! We all ate and ate and I think we all got sick. I know I ate five boxes of dates, one after the other ... such sweetness after the long lack of sugar. My friend ate too much and was in hospital for two weeks. On arrival in Iran we'd been weighed; I was ninety pounds."

Action this day
On July 13, 1943
Prime Minister to General Ismay for C.O.S. Committee

The time has come to bring the Polish troops from Persia into the Mediterranean theatre. Politically this is highly desirable, as the men wish to fight, and once engaged will worry less about their own affairs, which are tragic. The whole corps should move from Persia to Port Said and Alexandria. The intention is to use them in Italy.... *The Second World War, Volume V, Closing The Ring,* Winston S. Churchill.

Lieutenant Conrad (in eyeglasses) visited the Polish officers who were convalescing at a Polish Army Hospital in Italy in 1943.

"In North Africa, as part of the Eighth Army, we went from trying to survive in below zero weather to experiencing intense desert heat. The other troops were in tropical gear but we started off in wool battle dress and our silly brass insisted on 'necks buttoned up'. They learned!

"I was an artillery officer again, a battery commander with the 5th Regiment, 2nd Polish Corps. We were motorized right away and further training was needed.

"When the unit went to Italy I was on a course in Cairo and joined them a week after they'd landed. I found that my CO had lost an eye in battle and the officer who'd taken my place was seriously wounded. 'What am I coming into?' was my thought. Somehow the reality didn't seem as bad as my imaginings but of course, it was bad.

"I earned a reputation for being able to sleep through the noise of our barrages. Normally the twenty-five pounders would be fired in succession but once, just to see if I'd wake, they fired the four all together. I slept on."

Lt. Leslaw Konrad-Korzeniowski was involved in heavy fighting at Monte Cassino and other battles in Italy. His most frightening experience was swimming across a river with the Germans only 500 yards (490 metres) away concealed in a wheat field.

"Shelling and bombing didn't frighten me but I lived in dread of the sound of the German Spandau machine-gun."

For all his horrifying experiences and deprivations he feels the worst thing he faced in the war was going to tell a Polish mother that her only son of seventeen years, had been killed.

"The woman was not far away working in a Polish Field Hospital. The boy was my radio operator and a good one. He was so young, I felt like a father to him and this boy was one of the first casualties in my battery. It was such a heart-breaking thing to do, to go to a mother with the worst of news. I could have sent somebody else but I felt I had to go."

His wife, Maria, lived on in war-torn Poland doing whatever work she could find, and received no news at all of her husband's fate until the end of the war. First there were the Russians in her country and then the Germans for two years until the Russians forced them out and occupied Poland again. Asked which of the invading forces was the least objectionable, there was no hesitation. "You could have put them on a balance scale and it would not have moved either way!". As individuals she preferred the Russians.

The Polish lieutenant was demobilized in Britain after the war and stayed there long enough to take an electrical course and try his hand at a few jobs. It was during this period that he decided to Anglicize his name.

"I saw little future there. My younger brother was already in Canada and wrote that he liked it very much and for me to 'come over'."

His brother Peter had been in France as an exchange student when Poland was invaded. He had made his way to England and joined the Merchant Navy (like Joseph Conrad, a member of the same family) in which he served until the end of the war.

And so the ex-Polish soldier joined his ex-sailor brother in Canada and later on, after spending years struggling with government forms and rules he was able to fetch Mary from Poland in 1960. The couple had paid more than most as a consequence of Hitler's military adventurism.

Editor's Note: 14,500 Poles, including 8000 officers, were detained in three camps in the Smolensk region of the USSR. No word was heard from any of them after April 1940. Their fate became known as the Katyn massacre.

The Second World War, Vol. IV, The Hinge of Fate, Winston S. Churchill.

Leslie Conrad recently retired from employment with British Petroleum, Montreal and maintains his philosophy "to take life in stride and not to despair when everything doesn't go your way. It could always be worse." That he knows.

20

Canadian Girl in the A.T.S.

Born in Brampton, Ontario, she was twelve years old when her immigrant father had returned to England to work his legacy, the family farm. At eighteen, **Jean Bull** joined the Auxiliary Territorial Service (British Army) because "although the war was frightening, most of us felt we had no choice but to get involved in a positive way." Private **Jean Alice Bull** in uniform, 1943.

F{OR THE GIRL} from a sheltered life in the quiet Sussex village of Beckley, army life was a rude shock.

"The first three weeks of basic training at Guildford were the worst; being thrown in at close quarters with strange girls of every type and the being shouted at continually."

A group of them were selected and sent to Blandford, Dorset.

"We drilled and drilled, and learned to use rifles that kicked like the devil. We fired them at targets while standing up and while lying down. We marched with them. We ran with them. And most of all we cleaned them! I've never touched a gun since."

Then they were transferred to Blackdown near Aldershot where they took heavy artillery training.

"We were introduced to all the instruments we'd be using, theory, manual, how the guns worked, etc. We worked on height finders, predictors, radar, and as spotters. I saved my notebooks for years and later wondered how I'd ever made sense of it all. Aircraft identification was particularly hard for me.

"While at Blackdown I tried to transfer to a Canadian unit but was refused on the grounds that I was on active service. However, I did get permission to wear Canada flashes on my uniform.

"From Blackdown we were divided up and posted to Royal Artillery batteries. Thus began a series of moves, for the most part up and down the east coast.

"At Grantham, our first camp, most of the men were older or unfit for overseas service. We were twelve girls to a Nissen hut. With only a tiny stove in the centre, the huts were perishing cold in winter. Our major was young and tough and fanatic about cleanliness. Each time we moved into a camp he'd have us scrubbing everything in sight and when we left, the newcomers could eat off the floors. We hated all that cleaning but our battery added to its good reputation.

"The command post where we worked our instruments was away from the guns but near enough for us to hear the duty officer's commands. Through the tracking of our instruments, electric and manual, information was transmitted to the gunners. The adrenalin surged when we were hot on the track of a German plane.

"By night the canteen was alive with impromptu dances, bingo, and conversation – all frequently interrupted by air raid alerts.

"Periodically we were sent to Firing Camp. Concentration camp was our term for it! A unit was usually sent when they hadn't fired at the enemy for three months. Army redcaps stood behind us and watched every move as we focussed on and then shot at a sleeve trailing behind a plane. I think the redcaps had a contest to see who could yell the loudest. We'd about jump out of our skins at the commands it was a wonder that the plane wasn't hit instead of the sleeve.

"In Derby our guns were on top of a disused coal mine. When they fired the ground shook beneath us and we lived in fear of a cave-in, having visions of disappearing into the bowels of the earth, guns and all.

"On the overnight move from Derby to Sheringham, we began with a five mile march to the station; transport was

The A.A. Mixed Heavy Battery is seen in action. The guns were 3.7 calibre and were predictor controlled. All the gun crew had to do was to load the ammunition trays, then the rest (range, elevation, bearing, and fuse) was controlled by the predictor girls.

available for kit only. It happened to be my twenty-first birthday and on the train another girl and I slept in makeshift hammocks, cramped up there in the luggage racks. Anyway, it made it memorable. Once in Sheringham, we were billetted in a big rambling old hotel which faced the sea. It was February and cold, so cold that we slept with our clothes on. Next evening six of us went to the local pub to celebrate my birthday and arrived back five minutes late and singing. The major appeared in no time, temper flaring, but when we explained the occasion he let us go.

"At one time our camp was on farm property at Barrow-on-Humber. The farmer had spread putrid fish manure in nearby fields and the stench was incredible. Stomachs rebelled and worse still, our breathing was affected and we found ourselves choking. There was a fast unscheduled move out of there."

When Jean Bull left Canada she kept in touch through letters with a girl friend. Later, her friend's brother, Robert Barrett, came to England with the Queen's Own Rifles of Canada. He located Jean and they fell in love. In 1943, she was granted a two weeks leave and they were married in Beckley.

"My family surrendered their clothing coupons so that I wouldn't have to be married in uniform. And after the ceremony they gave us a surprise. Everyone followed us back to my grandmother's house where we were going to stay. The family had pooled their food rations for a lovely reception. That was the last time I was to see them all together."

While Private Jean Bull Barrett was stationed at Lowestoft the ack-ack guns were busy. Searchlights arced and criss-crossed, numerous guns blazed and tracers streamed skyward. It was difficult to know which batteries made the direct hits but she remembers that one night, combined efforts brought down three enemy aircraft.

Food was sometimes scarce at Lowestoft and once when she was near the end of the line-up, all that was left was boiled turnips. She hated them as a child but took as much as she could get that day. And then there was the phone call.

"During a lull in activity one night we were sitting at our instruments in the command post. Phones rang incessantly and suddenly I had the feeling that one ring was meant for me and said so to my friend next to me. She laughed and told me I was crazy but when I was handed a message she was as shocked as I was. That call was to inform me that my husband had been seriously wounded on the European battlefront. I couldn't go to him or do anything to help. It was so very frustrating."

On VE Day her unit was in Sherwood Forest.

"Like everyone else we had such a celebration that evening. The old forest rang with our songs and laughter."

No longer needed on anti-aircraft sites, some of the single girls volunteered for continental duty and the rest were transferred to the Ordnance Corps. Jean Barrett worked in a large warehouse alongside German prisoners-of-war. The Germans, who did the heavy lifting, were still under guard and the ATS girls were ordered not to speak to them.

Next she went to a camp at Bedford and worked with Italian prisoners who brightened the days with their singing.

"We were sorting sacks and sacks of army uniforms. It was filthy work and we wore overalls, caps and masks, and it was straight to the showers at the end of the day. I think some of the uniforms were re-cycled and others burned. I was glad that job didn't last long."

Jean Barrett was back in Guildford for demobilization in July 1945.

"When I left the army I missed the companionship of the girls terribly and took some time to adjust to civilian life. One thing I did not miss was being barked at and to this day I hate to be ordered to do anything.

"Being in the service opened my eyes to injustices and ugliness as well as to the joy and compassion of my fellow humans. And through the discipline and responsibility involved I grew up overnight."

Jean (Bull) and **Robert Barrett** live in Belfountain, Ontario. Her husband Robert, was twice wounded in action and then contracted tuberculosis. He was shipped home in 1945 on the hospital ship, *Letitia*. In March 1946, Jean, his war bride, returned to her native Canada aboard the same ship. When their first daughter was born they named her Letitia.

21

Modern Weapons

Following the 1944 disbandment of the Home Guard, **Ernest A. Woodward,** who is in the centre of the front row, worked with the 1359 Squadron, Air Training Corps.

HOME GUARD EPITAPH.

Never in the history
            of human endeavour
Have so many been
            buggered about
By so few—
            for bugger-all.

Early in the Second World War the Home Guard in Britain was known as the LDV (Local Defence Volunteers). In the blackness before dawn one morning, World War I veteran, Ernest A. Woodward, and another LDV were patrolling a lonely country lane in Chelwell, Nottinghamshire. On hearing footsteps coming toward them, "Halt! Who goes there?" went their traditional challenge whereupon a woman's voice screamed "Don't shoot, Mister! It's only us!".

Her fear of being shot was unfounded although a more suspicious type of prowler might well have been run through with wooden-handled medieval-style pikes. The pikes, similar to those last used by Cromwell's troops in the mid-seventeenth century, were the defence unit's only weapons at the hazardous period of threatened invasion.

Following WWII **Ernest A. Woodward** emigrated to Canada and prior to his death in May, 1985, was residing in Kelowna, British Columbia.

In the years when our Country

was in mortal danger

ERNEST ARCHIBALD WOODWARD.

who served   25 May 1940 - 31 December 1944.

gave generously of his time and

powers to make himself ready

for her defence by force of arms

and with his life if need be.

George R.I.

THE   HOME   GUARD

22

Resistance in Holland

Bren de Vries and Bernadina Anthing-Vogel in the fall of 1940, seated by a window that was taped to lessen the amount of flying glass during bombing attacks. **Bernadina Anthing-Vogel** was still in high school when she stood on the roof of her home in the early morning of 10 May 1940. Along with her family she was watching German paratroopers drifting down over her city, The Hague. With an ironic laugh, she recalls that her uppermost thought was "Good, there'll be no school today so I'll not have to write my Latin exam." Her friend, twenty-year-old **Bren De Vries**, had been mobilized into the Dutch army, his height qualifying him for the elite Queen's Regiment.

On 14 MAY WHEN their beloved Queen Wilhemina was safely beyond the reach of the invaders, the Dutch army surrendered. During the five days under attack, army and civilian casualties in Holland numbered 24,000.

For the next five years the majority of the Dutch people displayed a stoic courage with a determination for survival and eventual return to freedom. When the German army invaded the Netherlands it was efficiently aided by the large German fifth column already in Holland, as well as by 50,000 Dutch Nazis led by Anton Mussert. The Dutch army found itself disorganized and facing heavy casualties while fighting in small struggling groups.

Arthur Seyss-Inquart, the German-appointed Commissioner for Holland had been instrumental earlier in the betrayal of his own country, Austria. For the remainder of the war he carried out a rule of terror and ruthless oppression. Such measures involved systematic German looting of civilian supplies and harsh atrocities against the Dutch.

By April 1942, Germany had imported 200,000 Netherlanders as slave labourers for their war machine. By the end of 1942, some 2,200 Dutch had been executed or had died in concentration camps or prisons.

In retaliation against a general strike which began on 29 April 1943, Seyss-Inquart placed most of Holland under martial law. Great numbers of civilians were shot on sight and hundreds executed.

At the end of April 1945, relief supplies were trucked into 'No Man's Land', and dropped over besieged areas of Holland by the Allies. This followed a meeting between Allied representatives and Seyss-Inquart and saved the Dutch people from further starvation.

Dr. Arthur Seyss-Inquart was one of twelve top Nazis found guilty of crimes against humanity and sentenced to hang by Allied judges at the Nuremberg trials. His execution took place on 16 October 1946.

Bren de Vries remembers the blitzkrieg. "All that you thought was important or that you'd taken for granted, it was all gone or changed in just five days. Adequate food, clothing, the right to travel and your basic freedom, gone. For a while the shock of being defeated and occupied left us in a state of limbo but once people decided not to take it lying down, they found inner resources to draw on."

Small cells of Resistance fighters began to form, quite independently of, and for a long time without knowledge of, others. An Ondergrondsche cell would consist of four to eight individuals who were identified by numbers and rarely knew each other by name. Bren de Vries and Bernadina Anthing-Vogel belonged to separate cells. In September 1941, when they decided to get engaged, Bren felt he should inform his fiancee about the general nature of his activities. He found that she had already guessed that he was in the Resistance and they continued working with different cells until Liberation.

The catalysts propelling them into underground work had been similar. Bren de Vries had a longtime Jewish friend living on the same street. "He was a few years older than I, married with two small children. Only six weeks after the invasion a German squad car drove into our street and went to their house. They picked up my friend and his wife, and brutally kicked the children in their stomachs. We never heard of these friends again. Later, the children too, were taken away."

Bernadina had known another Jewish family who also had two children. The parents had been picked up earlier and then, one day the children were put aboard a train with other children and promised that they would soon be reunited with their parents. "When the train came to a certain bridge in Poland, the Germans blew up the bridge and did away with all those children."

For most of the Occupation Bernadina lived and worked in The Hague. Bren de Vries as student and Resistance fighter, was in The Hague for two years. Later his activities took him along the Ijssel River and to the towns of Deventer and Apeldoorn. During the final eighteen months of the war both young people were based in Amsterdam.

Unless Dutchmen between the ages of eighteen and forty-five were in agriculture, police, medicine, or some specific work for the Germans, they were removed from Holland as either prisoners of war or slave labourers. As forged papers permitted him to attend Agricultural College, Bren de Vries avoided exile.

Bernadina had become involved in the process of providing

falsified documents for patriots in need of them. And while listening to the BBC and Radio Oranje on her family's illegal shortwave radio, she would take the news down in shorthand. Next morning she'd carry the small pieces of paper to work hidden beneath the insoles of her shoes; at lunchtime she'd translate the shorthand ready for typing. Her mother owned an illegal printing press which was kept in a bedroom and used to run off illegal De Vryheid (Freedom) news sheets.

"We wore big swagger coats at the time and mine had a shawl effect that was double, ideal to hold the papers which we delivered to people we trusted. Some of our girls were caught and after interrogation at a local prison, they were sent to labour camps or wherever the occupation forces could use them."

Bren de Vries was engaged in diverse activities including sabotage. Cars, trucks, trains, any type of vehicle was blown up. And German soldiers were killed. The de Vries have a newspaper photograph of a high German official who, accord-

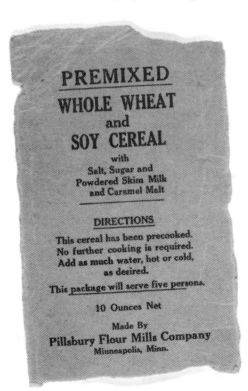

By agreement with Seyss-Inquart, the German appointed Commissioner of Holland, food was dropped by the Allies in April 1945 to prevent further starvation. Distribution was supervised by Dutch civil authorities, and issued on ration cards. Much of it was food no longer needed to feed American forces in North Africa.

ing to the caption, had met with an accident while travelling through Holland by train. Resistance fighters knew better. He'd been deliberately pushed off.

"My own first encounter was by chance. It was him or me. I'd been to Bernadina's home to listen to the London broadcasts and as I walked home after the 10 p.m. curfew, a German soldier challenged me. There was no way that I was letting him take me in for questioning so I took my chances and hit him. He ended up in a canal that carried sewage into the North Sea."

Following the midnight news, the BBC would broadcast coded messages to Resistance Forces.

"We'd receive instructions about rendez-vous with agents to be parachuted in, or about a plane that would be landing to pick up someone. Sometimes equipment would be dropped together with an instructor, usually from the Free Dutch forces, to teach us how to use it.

"In April 1941, there were a huge troop movement from the Atlantic coast towards the east. We were asked to transmit details regarding which units and equipment were on the move. We didn't realize it then but the Germans were already re-grouping to invade Russia.

"By the summer of 1944, we were well trained in all sorts of weapons and had plentiful stocks of Bren and Sten guns.

"Our Resistance cell managed to hide a small number of Jews and save them from deportation. Amsterdam Jews were rounded up and transported to a holding camp at Amersfoort, or sent to work in the Phillips factory at Eindhoven."

Bernadina de Vries had kept letters written to her by a Jewish girl friend detained at the holding camp along with her parents. The girl was permitted to send out two letters a month. Each was carefully written on one side of a small sheet of paper which carried strict instructions in German as to the exact number of words allowed per line, etc. In time the girl and her parents were all separated but were among those who survived the holocaust.

Under surveillance by the regular German army and SS troops, the Dutch patriots also had to be wary of their own 'quislings'. Most of the latter were in the Dutch SS or the Land Wacht, a collaborationist security force. "To us, these were rats of the worst kind because they were Dutch," comments Bren de Vries. "They'd stop anyone and commandeer anything, especially bicycles and food. People we knew were caught and executed, often more than one from the same family. Some held out under the tough interrogation, some broke, and some swallowed a cyanide pill supplied by the Resistance."

In August 1944, he was informed that his cell in Amsterdam had been infiltrated and that Germans would be around that afternoon to pick him up. He was given the name of a farmer in the village of Noorden who would take him in.

"I immediately set off on my bicycle with wooden tires and then caught a little tram drawn by a steam engine. I arrived at Noorden late in the afternoon and took supper with the family. So far, so good but in the evening the local doctor arrived with news that Germans were searching the next village, obviously looking for someone. We discussed whether I should stay or spend the night hiding in a rowboat on the lake. I stayed. It was around midnight when I heard the ominous sound of German army trucks. The farmer had no choice but to admit he had a young man in the house for I was sharing a bedroom with his two small boys.

"Footsteps were coming upstairs. I recall feeling relieved that a letter begun to Bernadina and lying on a table, contained nothing to cause suspicion. The German officer and the Dutch Nazi put me against the wall and went through my belongings. Interrogation in German had begun when suddenly, my pyjama pants fell down around my ankles. With a gun pointing at me, I didn't dare reach down and pull them up. They were examining my identity card (with its falsified information) again. The card itself was genuine because blank cards were stolen by the Resistance. Bernadina had prepared mine and I'm sure it saved my life more than once. I explained to them that my services were necessary to the district food production and with my degree in agriculture I was of special assistance to farmers. The card and my story must have satisfied them for they left. I pulled up my pants and breathed easier.

"Through the Resistance I received forty guilders a month, a fair amount at the time. Resistance also looked after the provision and distribution of free rail passes. Mine corresponded with my other 'official' papers."

Travelling on a streetcar without those papers on one occasion, he had a narrow escape.

"We were approaching a bridge and I could see the police checking vehicles up ahead. Knowing that a quisling would obey and stop anyway, I took a chance and told the driver I had no papers on me. I was lucky. He increased speed and kept going for three or four blocks beyond the bridge before stopping. As he slowed down I was able to jump off and disappear through the backyards of Amsterdam."

To Netherlanders, 5 September 1944 is known as Mad Tuesday. In the still-occupied part of Holland rumours were rife regarding the Allied advance and in Amsterdam word had spread like wildfire that The Hague and Rotterdam had been liberated. In a sudden surge of euphoria Dutch flags were hung from windows, and waved by the crowds rushing mistakenly toward the main highway to meet the Allies who were actually still in the vicinity of Antwerp. The confusion was such that even Germans and quislings were packing and leaving.

People pedalled bicycles indoor to generate enough electricity for reading lights. This man is reading the illegal newspaper, *Het Parool*.

"In our imaginations we could already see the quislings hanging from the trees but when the Germans came back they took revenge. From then until the end of the war turned out to be our hardest time and Mad Tuesday revenge was only part of it.

"We had neither heat, nor light in the winter of 1944. No gas, no electricity, nor even candles. We'd use tiny generators on bicycles and each person in a family would pedal away for a few minutes while another would read a book aloud. Another very real hardship was the lack of soap."

Following the Arnhem debacle, the most densely populated part of Holland was cut off and close to 18,000 persons starved to death. Food rations were dispensed from Central Kitchens and one person's weekly allowance of food consisted of one loaf of bread, six pounds (2.73 kilograms) of sugar beets and two ounces of skim milk powder. No butter and no meat. Bernadina de Vries remembers that through the winter those meagre rations were augmented for her family by five Swedish Red Cross parcels. The hungry and beleaguered Dutch were immensely grateful for the life-saving gesture. Prior to Liberation, Bernadina was to enjoy a period of temporary relief from extreme food deprivation.

"I had lost so much weight. I was down to eighty-five pounds (39 kilograms) and my family was worried. In January 1945, a few well-to-do Amsterdam families decided to send a group of children to stay with farmers in Friesland where food was more plentiful. I was lucky to be one of the two adults chosen to accompany the children. We went in an open truck and for my lunch I took along two slices of bread with a potato patty as filling. The patty had been made from potatoes that had frozen. When we went into a restaurant in Friesland we just couldn't believe that people would leave food on plates and walk away. Our poor kids from the city were on the verge of starvation and it was all we could do to make them sit quietly. They wanted to devour the left-overs and who could blame them. The children were distributed among the farms and I stayed in Friesland for six weeks.

"As barter for food I'd taken along silver cutlery and other fine presents we'd received at our engagement. I was determined to take back food for my family and to do this I'd have

During the 'hungerwinter' of 1944-45, Dutch people used bicycles to get food from the farmers, when they had some to spare.

to return in a truck with a certain type of cab structure so that the food could be hidden. The only way out of Friesland was across the dyke causeway and we'd face inspection. My permit allowed me to stay until 10 March but at that date there was no truck going out. I waited and waited. Then on 19 March, I naively went to the German authorities and requested another permit. But they remembered my unusual name and that I'd been there previously. Before it went any further I left quickly, thinking to myself, 'If I can't do it legally, I'll have to falsify the original permit.' That same night the farmers found me a truck with the only condition being that I provided the driver with black-market tobacco. The truck was transporting cheese to the Germans and I arrived home in Amsterdam at 4 a.m. with food treasures intact. Bacon, cheese, suet, skim milk and potatoes. All more valuable then than silver or gold.

"I still have that permit and it isn't difficult to see where I changed the 10 to 19. Thank God it was good enough to get past the checkpoint that night."

Tall Bren de Vries was by then weighing less than 110 pounds (50 kilograms) and thought of the food dropped by Allied planes in April, 1945 as 'manna from heaven'. The manna was army rations no longer needed in North Africa.

The ordeal was almost over but not quite.

"Many of our fighters were lost in the final days just before the Winnipeg Rifles arrived in Amsterdam. We'd decided that we'd take over ourselves but the Germans were still very strong; their backs were to the wall and we were engaged in fierce fighting."

Bren de Vries and Bernadina Anthing-Vogel were married in August 1945. A Canadian corporal saw that they had a few extras for the reception.

"We sometimes wonder now, how we did those things in the war" reflects Bernadina. "We were living not a day, but a minute at a time and every minute was precious. It proved a perfect base for our marriage because we'd learned what was really important in life. We have no time for petty troubles and complaints."

They emigrated in 1948, and became citizens of Canada five years later.

Still Bren de Vries had not quite left the strain of the Occupation years behind him. In 1950, he was driving through a small Ontario village on a quiet Sunday morning when a flashing light closed in from behind him.

"It was a sudden involuntary reaction. I froze and began to shake. In my mind at that moment it was the Landwacht or the SS after me. The Canadian policeman first asked why I was shaking and then told me that I'd been driving over the speed limit. 'Oh, Is that all!,' I answered."

> In 1957, **Bren de Vries** was ordained. As an Anglican priest he worked in several Ontario parishes while at the same time taking a full and responsible part in their community affairs. Appointed Port Chaplain, Quebec City in 1981, he administered the Flying Angel Seamen's Mission there with typical energy and enthusiasm, ably assisted as always by his wife, **Bernadina.** Although, on 1 January 1985, Rev. Bren de Vries retired from the active ministry, his active life continues. He and Bernadina reside in Baden, Ontario.

23

War and Love – A Soldier's Lot

Private Eric Hibbert, Black Watch (Royal Highland Regiment of Canada), on leave from Germany in England for his wedding in March 1945. **Eric Hibbert,** a nineteen-year-old textile printer of Valleyfield, Quebec enlisted in the Black Watch (Royal Highland Regiment of Canada) on 6 May 1940. Following two months of duty in Newfoundland, he returned to Canada and sailed for England with his regiment 3 September 1940.

While on foot patrol near Saltdean, Sussex in January 1941, he met a seventeen-year-old English girl **Joyce.** Here are a few unedited extracts from some 250 letters he wrote her during those 4 years.

20 February 1941

I've just come off guard again. I suppose you think we do nothing but guards, and honestly it was the most miserable night I've ever done. It started off by raining and ended up by Arctic weather. I almost froze to death. We have to get up at 4:30 a.m. tomorrow morning and go out for all day playing soldiers or something. They have just been around with blank ammunition so we're probably going to shoot each other instead of the Jerrys from now on.

1 March 1941

We had an awful time the three days we were on manoeuvres. We slept in barns which were still occupied by their righful owners – cows. And to make matters worse it rained two full days. I wish you could have seen me the second day out. We marched about eighteen miles in the pouring rain and my hair was hanging all over my face and I was drenched to the skin. I'm afraid that if you'd heard the language I used you wouldn't have thought much of me. Someone remarked that if they'd had a camera with them they could have made a fortune selling pictures to cartoonists.

12 March 1941

I was so mad when my pass didn't come through that I told the sergeant-major that the army was run by fifth columnists. I thought for a while of coming without one but I would only be further in the soup with the major and then I'd never get a pass.

17 March 1941

Don't worry too much about what I'd been doing because it wasn't anything really. I just happened to be late for breakfast and I got a couple of days for it. Can you figure that out, the country is at war and they crime us because we want to save the rations?

20 March 1941. Aldershot

We had an air raid up here last night. They didn't drop anything in the immediate vicinity but a couple of miles further down the road got plenty.

182

24 March 1941

I've had an awful time today with being so gloomy. The boys must have noticed it and they've been teasing the life out of me but I don't mind.

I wish we were coming back down there on our next move. I'll try my best to get down there again before we start moving. In case I can't make it, remember that song 'We'll Meet Again'.

30 March 1941

We had the honour of being inspected by the King and Queen last Wednesday. It was quite an event as a lot of the boys had not seen them before. We were standing out six hours waiting for them but it was worth it.

3 April 1941

I wish you could have seen me this afternoon when I was doing my washing. I had my sleeves rolled up, covered in soap suds leaning over a scrubbing board. I looked more like a washerwoman than a so-called soldier. And I was thinking about your aunt asking me whether we had our washing done for us!

9 April 1941

I don't know how I'm writing this letter. A couple of the boys are trying to kill each other with the boxing gloves on. Another one is playing his mouth organ with three others helping out with vocal ability. What a racket. It's worse than a circus.

20 April 1941

We landed back from a four-day scheme on the other side of Worthing last night and your letter was more like a gift after being out in the dirt for four days. We were out the night of the heavy bombing and being so near the coast, we had our share of thrills. Three bombs landed about 200 yards from one of our Companies and it was a miracle that no-one was killed. That same night Fergy and I were bedding down in an old barn alongside a railway track. Suddenly we heard a hissing noise and he said, "Get down." I said, "It's only a train," – and then the bomb landed in the next field – and I got down fast.

26 April 1941

I get teased from morning till night and the corporals have started looking at the postmark and shouting Peacehaven instead of my name.

Yes, it is a beastly war and there's many a time I wish I was on a ship sailing for Greece or somewhere. One gets so bored being stuck in this place (Aldershot) week after week. But if it goes on like this there'll be another Dunkirk in Greece and that will stop another chance for action.

2 May 1941

We had a swell time on the scheme this week. One of the drivers ran his truck into a ditch, turning it on its side. The sergeant-major went out looking but couldn't find him. The truck was full of equipmnent and the driver couldn't leave it. He was left out there for three days. All our blankets were on that truck and believe me, it was cold sleeping out on the Downs with no blankets, and no shelter of any kind, not even trees.

We are going on a 3 day route march next week. I can't imagine what I'm going to feel like after three days of marching. We're supposed to do 75 miles. I think I could have a lot more fun walking on the cliffs than marching on a highway.

9 May 1941

I was a little tired when I landed back but I finished the march without having to drop out at all. In fact, I didn't even get a blister. The march was actually 68 miles believe me plenty long enough on hard roads, with full pack on.

I wish they'd lift that awful ban off the Brighton area for the summer so that I could get to see you.

28 May 1941

I've been having a wounderful time. I was working in the kitchen yesterday and I peeled potatoes for 3 meals, 970 men each meal so you can tell how many I peeled. I dreamt of potatoes last night.

3 June 1941

I got an awful lecture today and I was lucky to get off without going up for it. The sarge told one of the boys to get 4 men to do a job. Two went, but Fred and I told him where to go and what to do as we didn't like being ordered by a private. Sarge figured out something for us to do and I've just finished counting out 5000 rounds of ammunition and putting them into Bren magazines.

1 July 1941

This being Dominion Day we were supposed to get a holiday but we've been scrubbing floors and cleaning windows. We'll be lucky if we get out at all today.

I'm so excited about getting out of this hole (Adlershot) that I didn't even feel bad when I landed back from leave. And I'm so busy thinking of seeing you, I can't write.

20 September 1941

Yes, I certainly would have liked to have been in the raiding party that landed in Norway. It must have been a lot of fun and as you said "a crack at Jerry". Anyway our chance will come one of these days and we'll probably regret it then. (I think I'd sooner do my attacking in Telscombe Cliffs).

26 March 1942

I heard that Jerry had dropped a couple of bombs on Newhaven. I was surprised to hear that he was bombing places where Canadians are stationed. Lord Haw Haw said that he wouldn't bomb the Canadians as they were a menace to the country and better left alone.

21 April 1942

You would have laughed Sunday night. I got on the bus and there was one of our boys from B Company on. Stewed as usual, he came over and sat with me. All of a sudden he let go with a YIPEE at the top of his voice and almost scared the life out of everyone on the bus. Being drunk he didn't mind but I was as red as a beetroot – everyone staring as if we were both drunk.

9 May 1942

We had to hand in all our blankets and we were left with nothing but greatcoats for the scheme. I got up about five o'clock this morning and it was so cold I gathered some wood and made a fire. Of course, as soon as I had it lit half the Company was up and crowded around it. It was just going nicely when we heard the drone of planes and then the bombs started dropping. That was Bexhill that got it this morning and from what we can gather from the farmers, they got pretty well smashed up. Anyway, as soon as the bombs started our officer said, "Put out that fire," so there was all my work gone up in smoke.

Fortunately kid, I have a little better news, we are supposed to be back for three days after this scheme so I'll likely be around to annoy you.

24 August 1942

So sorry I couldn't make it yesterday but you can guess who the first chance was given to. The boys who came back from the raid (Dieppe) were given leave first. And then there was a church parade yesterday morning so between the two I didn't get a pass.

Well, Valleyfield lost one of its boys in the raid. You remember the day of the War Weapons Parade in Eastbourne and the chap we passed at the corner near the bus station. He didn't return. No one knows yet whether he is a prisoner or otherwise. I hope he is only a prisoner because he's a swell guy.

24 October 1942

I had some very bad news earlier in the week. I received a wire to say mother had passed away last Saturday. I have been in a sort of a daze ever since. It came so suddenly. It's probably just as well that it happened fast, it saved suffering. I only wish I could have been there. It makes one feel alone when something like that happens and you can't do anything to help.

10 November 1942

We were out on a small exercise this morning and a smoke screen had to be laid down so the mortars were called on the job. It was carried out so efficiently by myself and another mortar man that we were highly congratulated on it. It's just like I always said, you can't keep a good man down, and I think it's time the army realized that I should be a general instead of a private.

22 August 1943
Of course I can't say anything as you know, but the NCOs were CB (confined to barracks) Friday night and that is why I couldn't phone. We couldn't have seen each other today because I wouldn't have been there to meet you. I don't suppose that is much of an explanation but I'm afraid it will have to do as these letters are censored. There's no canteen and no show so you can imagine what a thrilling time I'm going to have. Oh yes, you had better send me a couple of stamps if you want letters because we can't get any here.

2 September 1943
This dump is enough to make anyone feel that way (grumpy) so don't mind anything I say while I'm here. Last payday four of us marched into the post office. Four wires were sent and they all began the same way – please send $. I suppose you'll think us an awful lot but actually we're not. It's just that we all intend having a good leave when we do go, we're leaving nothing to chance.

21 September 1943
I want to be with you so much, I haven't been able to think of anything else since I left you. Still, I suppose there are millions more the same way so I guess I'll have to put up with it for the time being.

13 October 1943
We have to go through a gas tent this afternoon so I imagine if I do manage to get down I will be pretty sick and miserable.

29 October 1943
It took us twenty-six hours by rail and five by truck to get up here. Quite a ride eh, kid. Boy, what a hole this is. Even if anyone wanted to leave I doubt very much if they could get out. It's about sixty miles from the nearest railway station and twelve to the nearest village. I'm certainly glad that we're only

here for two weeks.

Actually, it's beautiful country. From pictures you showed me of North Wales it looks something the same. I think there are more hills up here though – and I used to think the South Downs were bad. We went up one this afternoon, 1700 feet. What a climb, it just about killed me. We had a beautiful view from the top and could see miles down the loch. I can't say which one it is. We also saw a couple of deer on the way up. And we went along the edge of Loch Lomond which looks like any other lake to me. We also saw Ben Nevis which is supposed to be quite a well-known hill over here.

I don't see how people could live out here in this wilderness, it's so desolate and dreary. Today was the first one without rain for weeks and weeks – that helps build our spirits! Oh well, I suppose I'll survive the two weeks.

11 November 1943

Talk about the bush, we are so far from civilization that all the birds have left. And there are seals in the bay that we used for training so you can tell the water was cold. We were in the drink four times in one day and every time it was like being turned into a block of ice. Can you imagine – making us jump in with Mae Wests (lifejackets) on – just to prove to us that they would hold us up.

The countryside is packed with deer up there, as many as twenty in a herd. Needless to say, we had a couple of feasts of venison which was absolutely delicious.

15 June 1944 (enclosure)
General Eisenhower's message to Allied Expeditionary Force.

Supreme Headquarters Allied Expeditionary Force

Soldiers, Sailors and Airmen of the Allied Expeditionary Force! You are about to embark upon the Great Crusade, toward which we have striven these many months. The eyes of the world are upon you. The hopes and prayers of liberty-loving people everywhere march with you. In company with our brave Allies and brothers-in-arms on other Fronts, you will bring about the destruction of the German war machine, the elimination of Nazi tyranny over the oppressed peoples of Europe, and security for ourselves in a free world.

Your task will not be an easy one. Your enemy is well trained, well equipped and battle-hardened. He will fight savagely.

But this is the year 1944! Much has happened since the Nazi triumphs of 1940-41. The United Nations have inflicted upon the Germans great defeats, in open battle, man-to-man. Our air offensive has seriously reduced their strength in the air and their capacity to wage war on the ground. Our Home Fronts have given us an overwhelming superiority in weapons and munitions of war, and placed at our disposal great reserves of trained fighting men. The tide has turned! The free men of the world are marching together to Victory!

I have full confidence in your courage, devotion to duty and skill in battle. We will accept nothing less than full Victory!

Good Luck! And let us all beseech the blessing of Almighty God upon this great noble undertaking.

21 June 1944
I want you to know that I have given Tiny your address so that if anything should happen to me in the future, he can let you know. As it is I've got to do the same for him. I only hope we don't have to make use of the addresses.

27 June 1944 (Folkestone)

Last night it was those awful doodlebugs. Never heard such a row in my life. A couple exploded and I swore the building was going up. All those down your way never had a thing on last night. It was terrible. Windows were broken in our billet and it knocked our blackout down but after a couple of hours it stopped and I got to sleep.

5 July 1944 (aboard a ship bound for France)

Sorry I couldn't keep the date but you know how these thing are. I had no choice in the matter. Anyway I think we were lucky to have had a few hours together before my leaving. It seems strange after all this time of waiting to get aboard a ship and know that you're really going places. I suppose this letter will be held up until we reach our destination.

12 July 1944

Nothing very exciting has happened to us yet – that is, nothing compared to what is happening to others. Apart from a little shelling and a few Jerry planes over, all has been quiet. We are up close to the front now and when I say quiet, I don't mean it in the true sense of the word. It's something like England when a doodlebug comes in – only this is continuous.

I am hoping against hope that this thing will soon be over so I can get back to you. You've certainly no worries about the fast French girls you told me to beware of – I haven't seen any yet.

24 July 1944

I have just got out of hospital. Nothing serious – knocked out by blast. Of course I had the shakes when I came to but there are so many fellows suffering from shock that it is common. I felt like an ass at first, to be in hospital with nothing wrong with me so to speak, but I felt better when I met others the same way.

I've got my second hook (stripe) at last, just before we went into the line. I should have said before we broke through the line. God, what a night that was.

I hope you can read this, my hand is still shaking and my mind isn't at its best but at least it will let you know that I'm still OK. I lost all my stuff except for what I had in my pockets so this will have to go ordinary mail.

27 July 1944

I don't feel too bad now, still at times I get a punchy feeling. I'd improve in health much quicker if I was convalescing in Sussex instead of Normandy. I suppose you will be busy with those doodlebugs but from what I see in the papers we get now and then, they are not coming over as often. I suppose Jerry's got a little more to occupy his mind these days – what with the Russians on the outskirts of Prussia and things in Germany going wrong.

5 August 1944

I've been going from camp to camp and for a while it looked as if I might be sent back to Blighty but no such luck. You see, my head got worse as time went on and finally I couldn't stand it any more and had to go to a doctor. There is nothing they can do so I'm at a work camp which is supposed to bring one back to perfect health. I don't think I will be here long. I'll stick it till I feel a bit better and then ask the Medical Officer to send me back up front. The only thing wrong now is terrible pains in the head which I think is helped along by the fact I can't sleep any too well.

12 August 1944

It's twenty-six days now since I had a letter. Yours was the last I got. So you can bet your socks I'm looking forward to some mail.

Anyway I'm still OK but if my head keeps on like it has yesterday I doubt whether I'll ever be fit for the front again. I'm thankful that is isn't as persistent as it was at first and I suppose eventually it will stop aching.

I've almost worn your pictures out from looking at them. No, actually they're as good as ever because I take care of them. I think I'd go wacky altogether if I lost my pictures. They're not as good as the real thing by far but better than nothing at all.

15 August 1944

I still haven't had any mail, twenty-nine days now.

I wish I could write a book on things I've seen over here, some people would feel sorry for themselves when

I'd finished. It's a shame the way some of the poor devils are being treated. Fellows who practically ruined their lives fighting for their country and can't even buy a packet of fags at our Canadian canteen.

I wish I could be with you right now. Wouldn't it be lovely to step off a boat, on to a train, and find you waiting at the station. I think I'd go batty with joy.

On 5-7 November 1943. Black Watch on Assault Training.

18 August 1944

On returning to camp after a strenuous day's work, I found seven letters waiting for me, three from my family and four from you. I let out an awful shout as though someone had given me a couple of weeks leave or something. I simply ate them up.

I'm afraid I'm going to be kept out of the line for a while yet according to the old boy. I told him I didn't like this place and wanted to get back to the battalion. He agreed that I'd be better off in my own unit but as he said, it's no use sending a fellow back until he's completely better, or he'll come out again being incurable the next time. So I have to stick it out but I've got a better job working at Ordnance and although it's hard work, I like it much better.

I am now a full-sized Private once more so you can address my letters accordingly.

From what I heard on the news the other night, the Canadian soldier is going to get a nice spot of cash on discharge, something in the neighbourhood of three hundred and fifty quid. [350 pounds and an English pound was worth $5.00 then.]

26 August 1944

I've at last found Tiny. On arriving at his camp I found that he'd gone to hospital for a check on his ears. I found him in the second hospital I tried. By then it was getting late and I had to walk back in the pouring rain. It was worth it to find him and have a chat with an old pal. I doubt whether he'll ever go back up, he's got two busted ear drums which take a while to heal.

I seem to have a fairly decent job now. At least it's doing something towards winning the war and I'm once again with the combatants.

Yes, it is quite true about the patriots shaving the heads of women 'entertainers' – as you put it. I've seen a couple myself but they usually walk around with a hat on.

31 August 1944

We've been doing well for eggs and milk in this new spot. The French-speaking boys have made friends with a number of farmers who have been very good with their eggs. I suppose they find it strange that soldiers are paying for things instead of taking them like Jerry used to do.

22 October 1944 (Somewhere in Belgium)
The weather had been just about the same as it was last week, raining and cold. You'd get a laugh if you saw us dolled up to keep dry. We've got waterproof pants, rubber boots, raincoats and rainhats which make us look more like fishermen than soldiers. It's awful around our section of the ordnance dump. We got stuck in a field when we first landed and with all the rain, trucks have churned it into soup. It tires one more to wade through that stuff all day than to do hard work.

22 November 1944
I can't give you any news as to leaves but the first time I see a padre I'm going to ask him about getting permission to be married. I think it is my best bet because if I just apply through normal channels it would probably take months.

What a country this is. It rained every day since I've been here and in my opinion it won't stop raining until I leave. It's about the most desolate place in the world, I'm sure – and even the people look as black as the sky.

24 November 1944
I'd give anything to be able to spend Christmas with you. We've never had a Christmas together yet, have we. Seems there is always something that keeps us apart. I wish old Monty would hurry up and finish this thing. Don't worry though, if they keep us apart another twenty years, I'll still love you.

27 November 1944
Last night I didn't have a cigarette to my name and this morning the weekly allowance came through, eighty fags, a bar of soap, and a real pint (half litre) bottle of English beer. I haven't touched the beer yet, I'm afraid I may not see another for six months. It's only the third English beer I've had since I left Blighty. We're supposed to get one a week.

194

8 December 1944

Action at last. I finally saw the padre and have done all I can towards getting permission to marry. Here's the things you have to do. First, see your doctor about a blood test. Then get a letter of character from a responsible citizen, a minister or a public official. Thirdly, you fill the part on Page 2 of the enclosed forms. When you get all this done, bung them all in an envelope and ship back to me on the double.

You'd also better see the minister and ask about the bans being read because I don't think I'll be able to give you much notice as to when I'll be getting leave.

22 December 1944

We had an awful night this week. Of course I can't tell you what happened but I soon found out my nerves wouldn't stand it for many minutes if I was to go back to the front. The thing that kept worrying me was whether I'd still be in fit condition to go on leave after it was over.

26 December 1944

We had a swell Christmas dinner, turkey, roast pork with all the trimmings, plum duff and all kinds of pies. I could have got good and drunk if I'd felt in the mood for it but I only had a whiskey and couldn't finish that.

I went in and had another blood test taken this morning. Talk about a butcher, I thought he was taking my arm off. Then he had the nerve to say, "Does it hurt?". I think he was suffering from a hangover because his hand was shaking like a leaf which made me jump.

16 January 1945

I saw *White Cliffs of Dover* last night. I thought it was a mar-vellous picture but as everyone said, not very good for the morale. It made everyone think of someone in England. It made me think of the day we sailed and how I sat on the deck and watched a certain stretch of the cliffs until I couldn't see them any more. I don't think I ever told you about Phil saying "Never mind boy, you'll be back some day." I guess he knew what I was looking at.

17 January 1945

Isn't it good to hear Warsaw has been liberated. I feel a lot happier to hear it than I did to hear any of the other capitals had been set free. At least they put up a fight before Jerry took the place and certainly suffered more than any of the other places. I think it's great news, myself.

16 February 1945

Don't worry about cars. If they're not available I'll fall the guests in in threes and march them to the church, a military wedding de luxe. Which do you thing would be cheaper, to hire taxis or a Southdown bus? We could have more guests with the latter.

28 February 1945 (Somewhere in Germany)

If everything goes according to plan I will be seeing you on the sixteenth of March. I hope the 19th is OK by you folks over there for the wedding day. Hope you understand about getting the special licence, I guess the minister will be able to help you. Sixteen days to go, no wonder I'm all excited.

3 April 1945 (Somewhere in Holland)

Sorry I couldn't write yesterday. Due to circumstances beyond my control it was impossibe. Those events happen more frequently now. As usual when things start happening the rain arrives. We had it all night and to make matters worse we had to take to terra firma, if you know what I mean. That's all I can say now.

13 April 1945

I definitely think it will be over by the end of this month. I believe I said June when I was on leave. When it does end I'm going to request to be sent home. I'm serious. I'm going to tell him I've been over here long enough and I want to go home to get things arranged for you. It might work and I've nothing to lose if it doesn't. He might think I've gone a bit mental, though.

17 April 1945

I was reading a piece in the paper today about someone saying the Germans shouldn't be treated so hard. Some soldiers had replied saying exactly what I said – that they didn't seem to be suffering. All healthy and well-clothed at others' expense. Some of the people who are for letting them off light should see a few things before they start talking. They probably haven't had a bomb for miles around where they live.

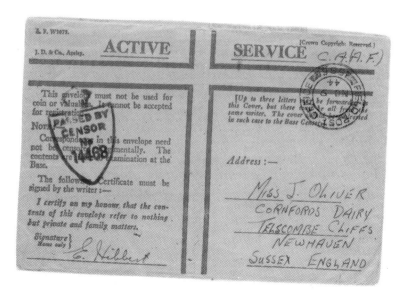

27 April 1945

This letter isn't going to be much because I'm too excited. I'll probably be in Blighty by the time you get it and I'll drop a letter or wire if I can't get away myself. Yes, the day has come, believe it or not, I'm going home. I'll probably be in Blighty by Tuesday or Wednesday. I can't believe it's true. After five years I'm going home at last.

I hope I can manage a few days in England so we can take a trip to London and see about getting you home.

Following a 48 hour leave in England, 8 to 10 May 1945, **Eric Hibbert** went home to Canada and was demobilized. His wife, **Joyce,** joined him in March 1946, and they have lived in Drummondville, Quebec ever since. Eric retired in June 1985 from his supervisory position at a local textile plant.

AIR

The first Mustang plane, the NA-73X, was developed in August 1940 in the United States. Then this prototype Mustang went into service and was shipped to Liverpool in October 1941. The Mustang became operational in the spring of 1942 with Canadians being the first pilots to use this plane in combat. The North American NA-73 Mustang I was a much used aircraft by the Royal Air Force in Britain.

24

Special Squadron, Special Duties

Flight Lieutenant **Robert McKee,** was in the Royal Canadian Air Force.

He was one of eleven children of an immigrant steelworker and his wife, the family having arrived in Ontario from Northern Ireland in 1923. Educated in Toronto and St. Catharines, young Bob found employment in Eaton's Toronto bakery and then spent a time as an itinerant salesman. By the late Thirties, he'd joined his father in the shipbuilding industry.

Coming from belfast, our family was British in outlook and could see the war coming. I volunteered for the regular RCAF and after taking a course as a PT instructor, promotion came rapidly with the outbreak of war and the resulting expansion. Only eighteen months after joining I was Chief Instructor of Physical Training at Trenton, holding the rank of Warrant Officer.

"Being a redblooded Canadian of Irish backround, I wasn't content to remain non-combattant for long. I reverted to the rank of sergeant and took navigator training at the age of twenty-four, a little older than average air crew. In 1943, I crossed to England on the *Queen Elizabeth*.

"At the end of courses in Southern England there came a request for replacements to a special squadron. Specifically, more mature types possessing above average map-reading skills were needed. And that was all we were told. Three of us from Central Ontario volunteered for whatever it was, and were accepted.

"My posting was to 296 Squadron, RAF. Its motto: 'Prepared for all things'. We were based at Hurn on the edge of the New Forest and I replaced a chap who'd become seriously ill. I trained with the crew for a few weeks before we went on operations. The other crew members were experienced, having recently returned from North Africa and airborne landings in Sicily. Our New Zealand skipper, Squadron Leader Roger Jamieson, was an aeronautical engineer formerly with De Havilland. Rejoining them after the war, he would head up the company in South East Asia. We five men would fly together for the remaining action-filled eighteen months of war, the only change in manpower being the addition of a flight-engineer when we switched to the bigger Halifaxes.

"On my first operation we flew into the Dijon area of France to make a drop of panniers containing special equipment. It wasn't the most routine of jobs – in fact a bit cloak and dagger, and I felt some exhilaration at really being in the war.

"So in we flew, low and slow in our Albemarle. We circled the target, received the Eureka beacon signal from the ground and turned on our lights. I was responsible for selecting the exact spot for the cargo drop. Meanwhile there was a passenger in the rear. He had his own special mission as con-

201

tact man and despatcher. It was official policy not to ask our passengers about their work, and they never offered any information. Should we be taken prisoner, the less we knew the better.

"Navigation lines on maps were not allowed. They too could fall into enemy hands and give too much away. Even so, I was surprised at the accuracy attained in our special deliveries made by dark of night. I found map-reading was much easier over there where everything was laid out in minute detail. At that time, Canada seemed too vast for that type of cartography.

"Following that first sortie there was another surprise for me when we walked into the de-briefing room in England. Hands were shaken with the congratulatory comment 'A very successful operation'. Agents or resistance people must have already reported results. 'Something else to keep us on our toes,' this new boy noted.

"On a typical night there'd be three or four planes going out from our squadron. We'd cross the coastlines at low altitude but making sure we were above the high-tension wires. It wasn't exactly your thousand bomber raid but often our operations coincided with heavy bombing twenty or thirty miles away and we could see the searchlights, flak, and fires in the distance as we sneaked in at a lower level. Although we often went in while the enemy was fully alerted, their attention was on the main raid and our operations seemed comparatively safe. Our pilots were all expert at low level night flying.

"A breach of security was suspected when we lost two aircraft in one night. Any security breach was particularly dangerous for agents who might land into the arms of the waiting Gestapo.

"Before my time, the Squadron Commander had been Freddy Pickard, RAF pilot and star of the film, *Target For Tonight*. He was killed during a raid on Amiens. They'd blown a hole in prison walls and the plane was downed when he stayed around to take pictures.

"Our Commanding Officer (CO) for a period was Group Captain Hockey, a man of inspiration and legend. One story had it that he'd flown assassins into Czechoslovakia by night, landed them and waited two days, well over their deadline.

The agents never turned up, so presuming them dead or captured, he was reputed to have flown his Hudson back across Europe in broad daylight. He was highly decorated and had this reputation for daring – and also for practical jokes. He was renowned for dropping Very Lights down the chimney pipes of Nissen huts full of officers – causing startling minor explosions in cast-iron stoves.

"Another CO while I was with 296 was Wing Commander Dave McMonies and he was Canadian.

"We were shot up ourselves once, in the undercarriage. And there was the time when returning from Norway, we radioed ahead that petrol was running out and we'd be lucky to get within thirty miles of the English coast. The navy sent out two destroyers, and searchlights were turned on along the coast. Luckily, we made it into King's Lynn but couldn't have gone round again. Gas was completely used up."

Bob McKee and crew flew from many different stations in England and Scotland depending on which occupied country was the target of operations. The crucial time for a crew was in the early flights. It was the same in Bomber Command, because the general rule was that the more experienced the crew, the longer they were likely to go on operating successfully.

Members of 296 and associated squadrons seldom asked for transfers. In addition to the valuable nature of their war effort with its underlying excitement and mystery, there were the tangible perks. These included extra leave money (donated by Lord Nuffield), operational petrol coupons, and special food rations; all benefits that young fliers were loathe to give up.

"Social life took place on short trips to London. From December 1943 until September 1944 my longest passes were for a scant two days. To make the most of the time we'd board the train complete with our 'wakey-wakey' (benzedrine) tablets. We'd take in one of the many good live theatre shows and then party into the night at one of the after-hours clubs. The next day we'd do the rounds of the service clubs looking for friends. Then it was back on the train. Hotels were used for a short 'crash' sleep and a bath.

"I'd like to stress that there was a lot less heavy drinking and

RAF planes (Halifaxes and Gliders) are lined up ready for take-off to France and the liberation of Europe on the evening of 6 June 1944.

'girlying' among aircrew than popularly believed. They were not on the whole, predisposed to habitual riotous living. They knew the necessity of staying sharp in order to stay alive. Of course we had our good times and romances in so far as the restricted lifestyle and priorities allowed.

"When an op was coming up for our crew we'd be required to stay on the station, usually for forty-eight hours before hand. Then closer to the flight, we'd be introduced to the agent or agents who'd be parachuting in. It was a matter of getting acquainted and likely lessened tension all round. Some of them had foreign accents and some spoke impeccable English. For the sake of security, we didn't behave any differently after being alerted but it was natural to feel a little stress until take-off. Again for security reasons, we were not always sent out from the same airfields. Many a time we'd open an envelope, proceed to the designated place and stay overnight, having no idea until briefing as to where we'd be going.

"Sometimes when we were to drop an agent, we'd carry 500 pound bombs and take a run at a target in the vicinity of the drop. We'd try to find a bridge or railway line or the like. There was no question of indiscriminate bombing.

"The agents were a varied lot of individuals but you knew

they were all made of strong stuff. There were a surprising number of British schoolteachers of continental backgrounds among the passengers. A British army captain who'd been raised in France would be dropped over there and a few weeks later, he'd reappear in our mess – as though nothing had happened. After the war he told me that his return Channel crossings had been made by fishing boat. My guess had been submarine. I watched French para-commandos, who wore a skull and crossbones insignia, practice unarming one another with the attacker wielding a lethal-looking knife. I watched in fascination – and measuring the risks, shuddered. My most vivid impression of an agent preparing to leave involved a little fellow I presumed to be a courageous Jew. He was to be dropped in the Vienna area by another crew and before he put on his jump suit there was no missing the yellow Star of David on his back.

"They'd been familiar with a locality's idioms and colloquialisms and French-convent-educated Irish girls were among

Flight/Lieutenant Robert McKee (on the right) talked with other Canadian airmen prior to the briefing on details of the Rhine crossing airborne assault in March 1945. Also in the group were Flying Officers, 'Eli' Eliason Mozart, Saskatchewan; 'Buck' Drever, Turner Valley, Alberta; and John Atkins, Toronto; all at Earls Colne, Essex, England.

the women agents. A personal regret is never having known the real name of one attractive young woman in her mid-twenties. Being a nosy so-and-so by nature, I managed to find out that she had represented her country in the 1936 Olympics, probably in swimming – but that was as far as I could get.

"I've often wondered what happened to the German officers we dropped. They practiced their Nazi salutes while waiting. Each was closely watched by a heavily-armed commando who issued them with bullets for their pistols immediately prior to their jump. I've since read that they were anti-Hitler but our people were taking no chances with them. Whatever their nationality or their business, we did our best to see that agents made it safely through the first leg of their missions."

In addition to their secretive incursions into enemy air space, on D Day Squadron 296 supplied three pathfinder aircraft and eight others towing gliders as part of the initial wave of airborne troops; then they towed in a further nineteen Horsas later in the day. At Arnhem they towed in twenty-five gliders on the first day and twenty-one the next. All without loss. Supply drops to resistance forces were again resumed and their Halifaxes would take part in the Rhine crossing. At the end of the war 296 Squadron flew troops into Norway and Denmark, and transported released prisoners of war back to the United Kingdom.

Bob McKee had been promoted to Flight-Lieutenant and his final wartime op was to Oslo, Norway. Germans were still in command of the airfield but their Halifax landed in a pre-arranged place and took out several important civilians.

"I am only sorry" states McKee, "that more has not been told about the contributions and exploits of the many Canadians who flew in these special squadrons and who worked so closely with and yet apart from those agents. If I had the chance to be young again, I'd opt for similar duties where hopefully, one wouldn't be totally under the control of computers."

Squadron Leader **Robert N. McKee** retired from the RCAF in 1965. Among his accomplishments in the Force was his writing of the manual, *A Guide to Airmen;* its instructions being a case of "Do as I say, not as I do", he hastens to explain.

Having spent some fourteen years instructing in Physical Training, Navigation, Management, and Electronics, he was well qualified for a teacher's certificate on return to civilian life. For six years he taught high school in Kelowna, British Columbia where he now lives in active retirement.

25

Close Shaves and Steady Nerves

Across the St. Lawrence River from Quebec City and twenty miles down the road from Levis is Ste. Claire, **Philippe Bernier's** birthplace. Flying Officer Philippe Bernier sat for this photograph in 1945.

Bᴙ ᴛʜᴇ ʟᴀᴛᴇ Thirties he was living in Drummondville and working at the Celanese textile plant. Most of the factory administrators then were from the British parent plant and young Bernier knew that in order to advance his career, he would have to improve his English. Immersing himself as much as possible in the language, he boarded with English-speaking people and took private lessons. Along with anglo-phone friends he travelled regularly to Trois Riviéres for flying instruction on Piper Cub J2s and J3s. When he decided to volunteer for war service, his application went to the RCAF.

"I chose the RCAF because I'd received my private pilot's licence in 1939. And because I loved flying. I realized that in the RCAF I'd be provided with the best in planes and instructors. My English wasn't perfect but I was persistent in trying to join and in December 1940, the air force decided to take a chance on me."

He was posted first to Moncton, where he flew Fleet Finches and then to Trenton where he became an instructor on Tiger Moths, Harvards, Wellingtons, and Mosquitoes.

On 15 April 1943, he was one of 105 flight crew officers sailing from Halifax aboard the *Amerika*, a Danish vessel sailing under the British Red Ensign but retaining her Danish captain, Christian Nielsen. The forty-two ship convoy slowly zig-zagged its way through the blustery North Atlantic towards Britain. But evasive tactics failed to deter U306 and Kapitan-leutnant Claus Von Trotha. On 21 April the *Amerika* had been selected as their prey. The convoy was in mid-ocean.

"It was between eight and nine in the evening and six of us were playing poker in the lounge when the first torpedo hit, almost immediately followed by a second. Lights had gone out instantly and men were yelling for others they knew. And I remember the sound of someone crying. I edged my way outside and came to a lifeboat station where a boat was being launched from above. It failed to stop at the stations and plunged straight down into the water. So I found my way to my designated station and jumped into the lifeboat being loaded there.

"It was lowered swiftly, and carried two sailors and nine airmen. As it hit the water we were swamped by giant waves which poured over our heads. Fortunately the lifeboat was

Philippe Bernier is in the centre of these pilots wearing their 'teddy bear suits' for warmth as they trained in open cockpit Tiger Moth aircraft which were fitted with skis, Moncton, New Brunswick, 1940.

equipped with special floats and did not overturn. The sailors rowed away from the stricken *Amerika*.

"Wearing life-jackets over sea-soaked uniforms and shivering in the snow and wind, we clung to the wooden seats and waited. Not knowing for what. 'How long could we last before exposure finished us,' I wondered. 'Where was the convoy, was it steaming ahead, or scattered? And how many ships sunk?' We heard later that the *Amerika* and Captain Nielson had gone down within thirty minutes of being hit.

"After about three hours we heard voices. My first thought was that the U boat had surfaced and was coming to pick us up – or more likely to pass the machine gun. Thank God it was the Royal Navy corvette HMS *Asphodel*. They took us aboard and delivered us to Greenock, Scotland. The *Asphodel* itself, was to be sunk by a U boat off Cape Finisterre on 9 March 1944.

"At an RAF station we washed and shaved and were given new uniforms. And that same night we were on a train to London where we told all we could about the torpedoing. I was one of only seventeen RCAF officers rescued and the sole survivor of the poker game. Young, intelligent and highly trained, the others had all disappeared in mid-Atlantic. I could only think that I was extra lucky and for some reason, meant to survive. I did not dare dwell on the horror of it."

Phil Bernier was sent to Bournemouth next where he filed claims for his lost possessions. The young pilot officer arrived there in time to witness hit and run raids by Focke-Wolf 190s. In these sneak daylight attacks on southern coastal towns, the fighter-bombers would fly in low over the Channel to avoid being tracked by radar. They'd unload their bombs on a prominent target, machine-gun busy streets, and be off out to sea again – often before warning sirens had sounded.

Phil Bernier was given two weeks of 'survivors leave' and then went straight on operations. He flew first with 407 Squadron known as the Demon Squadron, and then with 418, the City of Edmonton Squadron. He spent two years with RAF Coastal Command hunting for U boats and carrying out shipping strikes.

He came to regard being caught in the hub of a mass of searchlight beams or being the target of anti-aircraft fire, as routine hazards. Soon he was to have a second brush with sudden violent death while he was piloting Wellingtons out of Haverfordwest in Wales. Bernier was captain of a crew of six whose night patrols took them into Bay Biscay skies. They were using radar screens for detecting the enemy and this special new equipment could pick up any surface or air craft up to forty miles distant. Any craft encountered in the Biscay area then was almost certainly enemy.

"It was 9 p.m. on 14 November 1943, and we were sitting on the runway loaded up with fuel, torpedoes, and bombs. As we waited for the signal to take off on night patrol, another Wellington was coming in to land. Suddenly her pilot lost control and she veered right into us. Our plane's undercarriage collapsed and that was immediately followed by explosions and fire. I scrambled out as fast as I could through the hatch above my head. The navigator, badly burned, got out somehow through another hatch. The four others were killed.

"Jim Anderson, the RCAF navigator was hospitalized for a year before being sent back to Canada. I spent Christmas and

New Year in a Cardiff hospital recovering from facial and wrist burns. My hands were saved because I'd been wearing flying gloves. Once again I was amazed at my luck and thankful to be alive."

Only six weeks after the tragic accident, Phil Bernier was back with Coastal Command flying Beauforts and Beaufighters on night patrols.

"My navigator was Anthony Timpson, RAF. We got along very well and crewed together for the next eighteen months."

Before long the two men would be switched to Mosquito bombers based at Blackbushe, south-west of London. Then in April 1945, after just two weeks duty in Belgium, Flying Officer Philippe Bernier returned to Canada. His tour of operations was complete.

Thirty years later, fond memories of wartime Britain and her people prompted him to return for a visit. Madame Bernier, their daughter and son-in-law accompanied him. He had planned a surprise for Anthony Timpson whom he had not seen since 1945. Son-in-law Daniel, then a Toronto heart surgeon was his assistant.

The Timpsons still lived in the house near Manchester

Flying Officers Bernier, Bullman, Warren, and Timpson did some off duty map reading in Langham in 1944.

F/O Phillippe Bernier and friends cycled to a farm near Crosby in June 1944 for fresh eggs.

where the Canadian pilot had been entertained on wartime leaves. Daniel telephoned the ex-navigator business man and presented himself as a Canadian reporter looking for Second World War stories. He explained that he had heard that Mr. Timpson had flown with a Canadian pilot and would like to talk to him about his experiences. Anthony Timpson graciously agreed to see him.

At the pre-arranged time the two Canadian men turned up at the Timpson home. A camera-festooned Phil Bernier was introduced by Daniel as Mr. Patenaude, his photographer who knew no English. They all shook hands and went in to sit by the fireplace that Bernier remembered well, and Hilda Timpson served them tea.

"Then my son-in-law, Dr. Daniel Bonneau, began asking questions and taking notes. When Anthony spoke about his Canadian pilot by name, Daniel broke in with feigned surprise, 'Bernier, he was a French Canadian?'

'Yes, he lives not far from Montreal.'

'Well', said Daniel, 'in Canada we hear that French Canadians are not very serious and like to drink a lot.'

'Not Captain Bernier! He was a steady and sensible sort and a fine pilot.'

"Of course it was hard for me not to laugh because I under-stood it all. Especially when I was taking pictures and my ex-navigator turned to his wife and said seriously, 'Hilda, don't you think Mr. Patenaude looks a bit like Phil, my pilot?' They were both looking at me so I quickly asked Daniel in French, 'What did they say?' and that seemed to put them off the track. When we told them who we really were, we all had a good laugh. 'You were lucky' Anthony told me, 'that I spoke so well of you.' and we laughed again. We spent a happy two day get-together."

In 1962 **Philippe Bernier** joined the municipal administration of Drummondville as a alderman. In 1965 he was elected mayor. Returned in five succes-sive elections, he resigned from the mayoralty in 1983. He still flies, holding a commercial pilot's licence, and is qualified as an instructor on night flying and on seaplanes. "And ready", he says, "to serve his country again should the need arise."

26

Red-Letter Memories of an Air Gunner

Born in Hawk Junction, Ontario, **Martin Schellin** volunteered in February, 1941 at North Bay, Ontario. He was eighteen and chose the RCAF. Flight-Sergeant Martin Schellin, 407 Squadron, North Coates, England 1942.

MY DAD HAD A friend, 'Jock' Jarvis, who flew for Northern Development on fire patrols; he'd been a WWI pilot and often talked flying. This influenced me and I'd take off for 'The Soo', Michigan to clean hangars so that I could have free flights in Taylorcraft. It seemed natural that I should join the Air Force.

"My RCAF training progressed through security guard at 13X Ammunition Depot at Angus, to wireless and gunnery training on Fairey Battle and Avro Anson aircraft, to the Wings Parade at Mountainview, Ontario in August 1941. I passed out as Wireless Op/Air Gunner Sergeant and finished the war as Warrant Officer I.

In Britain active service was not all work and Martin Schellin recalls some of the lighter moments.

"Operational training and flying took up much of our time. Usually we made close friends among our own and other air crews. We might be sleeping while our friends were flying and vice versa so we tended to stay around the Mess a good deal. Most of us tried to grow an RAF moustache and took to smoking a pipe so as to look older.

"When my first leave came up, like so many other foreign servicemen I headed straight for London. From the Beaver Club I located a good hotel, unpacked, enjoyed the luxury of a private bath, and called for my No.1 uniform to be pressed. I visited a barber, sharpened up on London landmarks, had a meal and took in a show. Back to the unusual pleasure of a private room and quiet to write a card home telling them that I was in London at last.... and tactlessly mentioning the contrast with the sticks of Northern Ontario.

"Next morning it was round to the RCAF Accounts Section at Lincoln's Inn Fields to draw my deferred pay. The large five pound notes were a surprise but sure made me feel prosperous. On to the Beaver Club to taste real Canadian donuts and real coffee again.

"I was living high travelling by taxi because I was scared of the London Underground, having this vision of myself going round and round under the city for the rest of my leave. But I recall the day I conquered that. I followed two Polish Air Force officers. If these guys can travel on this terror, I reasoned, a Canadian should be able to manage. Then amazed at the ease of travel, I discovered a bonus. Young ladies were reading CANADA on my shoulders and it was fun to get them to talk so that I could enjoy their delicious accents.

"I began to explore London but after three or four days on my own, I was missing my crew and thinking of returning to camp early. Then at the Beaver Club I ran into some guys from my home town. In the Ontario Regiment (11th Armoured), they were returning to billets near Brighton that same day. I grabbed a taxi, packed my case, and joined them on a train for Brighton. All the carriages were full and it seemed fun then, to sit out in the corridor for the sixty-minute journey.

"My friends reported in at Roedean, the famous girls' school where they were quartered. Unfortunately the girls were gone. It was a lovely place set in lawns between the sea and the South Downs, exactly what I needed to calm my whole being so I spent my days sunbathing and relaxing. But I *was* on leave and the nights were a different story. We'd be off to Brighton and Sherry's Ballroom on West Street. Sherry's had a great floor, a balcony, two bands, and plenty of 'popsies'. It was there that I first heard Ivy Benson and her All Girls Band, a top attraction who played well. The place was a magnet for us guys. I even tried my luck at a tea dance in the afternoon but that was too quiet for me.

"On that leave I spent one night on duty with Royal Observer Corps men down there. They kept track of our own and hostile aircraft.

"Eventually I returned to the London hotel for a final night of luxury before rejoining the squadron. Funny, I was excited and happy about getting back to flying, being with my crew again, and comparing leave experiences (with a little harmless exaggeration). We decided that in future we'd go on leave as a crew and have even more fun.

"On return from leave there was always the dreaded question to ask. What losses had the squadron taken while we'd been gone? And there was some small envy for the guys who'd continued flying and therefore pulled ahead of us in ops completed.

"At the time we certainly enjoyed the company of girls but so many of us were between nineteen and twenty-one, not looking for permanent relationships. When planes were listed missing, we were touched by the sorrow of many an Air Force wife living near camp. Some older crew would get married or closely involved but the young crowd usually made its way to the local pub, learning English drinking songs and teaching civilians Air Force games. The latter seem silly as hell now but were a real part of life then. The Air Force boys were on the whole a pretty well-behaved bunch and were spoiled by the landlords. The majority conducted themselves reasonably well in order to stay fit enough to fly. Okay, we did drink and sometimes too much but that was almost always in our own Messes; often operations had been cancelled at the last minute, it was too late to go to town, and the sudden release of tension was excuse enough for a squadron bash. It didn't take many beers or pink gins to see us merry; bar stewards or batmen would escort us safely to our bunks. Tomorrow was a hundred years away.

"Mail arrival was always a highspot. One letter, re-directed from home, gave us many laughs and I pinned it up on our board. It was from the RAF in answer to my 1940 application to join up. When I got the letter I'd already been in England for over a year as air crew! Most of us had left girl friends back home and letters came thick and fast the first few months, then eased off until we realized that time and affections had marched on. Although I don't remember getting any Dear John letters, I do remember how foolish but proud I felt when my dad wrote to my Flight Commander asking whether he could explain why I wrote so few letters home. I understand now but at nineteen, priorities were not the same.

"Quite often RAF boys would invite us to spend a leave with their families. An invitation at Christmas was particularly welcome. I enjoyed the warm close feeling and the chance to go to Midnight Mass with a family again, hearing the priest say special prayers for our comrades. And the fun of teasing a young sister, then finding an apple pie bed – while catching her giggles in the hall. And Boxing Day was great – especially when aunts and uncles arrived and put on an impromptu concert. Yes, I enjoyed the English hospitality. It made the cold and dangerous job in the air easier to take and the happy memories are still with me."

Following operational training in England, Sergeant M.

This is the Halifax Mark III bomber, a *P Popsy*, in which Flight-Sergeant Martin Schellin flew on operations out of Linton-on-Ouse as a mid-upper turret gunner. His Majesty King George VI and royal party greeted the station commanders of No. 6 Bomber Group prior to holding a field investure for the Canadian air crew, at Linton-on-Ouse, 1944.

Schellin would experience over three years of the cold and dangerous job in the air. In November 1941, he joined 407 Squadron to fly in Hudson aircraft as a replacement air gunner. The squadron motto: 'To Hold On High' from 'Flanders Fields'.

"I completed one tour with Coastal Command attacking enemy shipping off the Dutch coast until we were all but wiped out. We re-grouped at Wick, Scotland where we converted to Wellingtons. After a period of anti-submarine work on the western approaches, we moved to southern England and patrolled the Bay of Biscay out of the RAF station at Chivenor in North Devon."

Though qualified for a posting home, like numerous other Canadian air crew he requested to stay on operational duty. Schellin was then seconded to 320 Squadron of the Netherlands Naval Air Arm 'to have a rest'. 320 Squadron was converting to Hudsons and officially F/Sergeant Schellin was instructing air gunners. He found himself on operations as well.

During this period a young English girl had won his affections and in September 1943, they were married.

It was another happy day in February 1944 when he was posted to 408 Squadron, No. 6 Bomber Group, RCAF at Linton-on-Ouse in Yorkshire. He tells here about one particular bombing raid but such exercises were repeated, sometimes two and three times a week, over and over again, until the men completed their tours (usually thirty operational flights), could not take it any more, or were posted wounded, missing, or dead.

"I hate like hell to talk about my own efforts. I'm a survivor and every day is a bonus for me. As a gesture to the memory of my aircrew buddies I shall try and leave an impression of what it was like on a typical bombing raid in those days. Days when heroes were everywhere; from schoolboys to grandmas – they could be found doing their best for final victory. I shall try and tell it the way it happened. No line shooting.

"I am still F/Sgt. and have just joined the crew of *P Popsy* as mid-upper gunner. We are flying a Halifax MK III with Hercules engines. Armament is one Vickers gun in the nose, four Browning guns in the mid-upper turret and four in the tail turret, with a Vickers gun free-mounted on either side to be used by the wireless operator or bomb aimer in an emergency. We usually carry 250 pound armour-piercing high explosive bombs, plus incendiaries and photo-flash flares, and at least a thousand rounds of ammunition for each gun. Add to that the fuel and oil, and finally the seven-man crew.

"Early in the afternoon we are required to report to our flight office in the hangar where we are advised that operations are 'on' and briefing will take place at 1600 hrs. We go back to our billets, bath and shave, and change our clothes. Then we make our way to the large Nissen hut for the briefing. Folding chairs face a raised dais holding a speaker's desk. The wall at the rear of the platform is covered with a huge map of Europe.

"Small groups of flight crew members drift in. They're laughing, talking, or just walking along deep in thought. Meanwhile life on the station continues as normal. When we are all seated, the Flight Commander, Armament Officer, Meteorological Officer, and Intelligence Officer come in. The meeting is called to order and the briefing begins.

"Tonight the target will be Dusseldorf, a manufacturing town about three hundred miles from our base and lying between Essen and Cologne in the Ruhr. The Ruhr, known to us as Happy Valley, is heavily defended with searchlight, flak, and night fighters.

"We have our Operation supper. The Operation meal is always bacon and eggs and normally served on return. But we have a WAAF Messing Officer who thinks it unfair that the boys who don't come back miss their fresh eggs – so we're given ours before we leave. Bless her.

"It's time to dress in heavy longjohns, battledress, white wool roll-neck sweater, and silk gloves. Then it's into the leather flying suits, boots, helmets, and parachutes. As I sit outside the flight office with the rest of the crew, I'm also wearing a silk stocking around my neck – for luck. We are driven out to our aircraft in a fleet of three-ton Bedford trucks. With cheers and Churchillian salutes we take leave of the other crews who will be flying with us. Tonight is maximum effort.

"In the evening shadows she waits. Our *Popsy*. Beautiful to us. We take our positions aboard and start our individual rituals to ensure our plane is top line. We start engines, check turrets, bomb load, ammunition, even our coffee flasks and escape kits. We stow our parachutes. Finally we join the taxi rank and take off. We circle the field to gain operational height and head east, crossing the English coast at Great Yarmouth. At about 16,000 feet we cross the Dutch coast near Ijmuiden, heading for just south of Essen.

"We meet light flak over Holland and ahead of us searchlights are combing the sky. I am now traversing my turret continually, watching for exhaust flames that could be fighters waiting to jump us. Suddenly I see winking tracer coming in fast on the port side. I hold fire as he grows larger in my sight for I want to avoid waste of ammo. He approaches fast. It's an ME 110 twin-engined night fighter. I give him a three or four second burst, see flames and give a longer burst, about ten seconds. He breaks below us, diving fast. Meanwhile two of his comrades had jumped the tail gunner and raked our tail fins with machine-gun and cannon fire. We are already taking what evasive action we can by cork-screwing and losing height quickly but we are pretty well exposed in the searchlights ahead of us. Then suddenly it's quiet except for the steady roar of our four engines. After having the Brownings blasting away only inches from your ears, the engine noise alone is music.

"Score: One 'flamer' for us and 'one probable shot down'.

"The skipper checks out the crew and we are all okay except the rear gunner. He is assisted from his shattered turret and laid on the rest-bed amidship. The bomb aimer takes over in the tail turret as lookout, it is no longer serviceable otherwise.

"Now we are only five minutes from target area so the navigator takes over the rear turret and the bomb aimer goes forward to his duties and drops our load on the target indicators. It looks like a gigantic bonfire from up here and makes me wonder what extra damage our bombs could possibly do. The skipper keeps the ship on even keel while the raid photographs are taken. At last I breathe easier for I can feel we're making a climbing turn in order to join the homeward stream.

"Our tail gunner has been given a shot of morphine and is unconscious. With aid of my flashlight I look at his ashen face behind the oxygen mask, and I say a prayer or two for him.

"The return trip is nerve-wracking. Our hydraulic system has been ruptured, tail turret knocked out, tail fins damaged, main petrol tank leaking with the ever-present danger of fire, and our tail gunner may be dying. All this has been taking place in extremely cold and dark conditions but it is only when the excitement eases off that you begin to notice the frost and how damned tired you are. However this is the very time that the German 'intruders' operate. They infiltrate the swarm of returning bombers and jump you just when you may be thinking how lucky you are to have completed another op. So one must work harder, traversing the turret and straining the eyes, hoping that luck will hold for at least this trip.

"Eventually I hear our skipper requesting landing permission and advising base about the tail gunner and possible aircraft damage. Permission to land is given at once and we prepare by losing height. More trouble. The flaps won't work and *P Popsy*'s wheels are not locking down. We receive a red flare from the ground and are advised to land at a satellite 'drome ten miles away. So we approach the emergency 'drome which is really just a flare path with a crash crew standing by. We are coming down. The skipper orders us to take up ditching position behind the main spar, hang on and pray.

"We start counting seconds and waiting for the crash.... but our skipper, Flying Officer Barber, really lays it on the grass. Tail first, we are slicking along about ninety miles an hour, no brakes, everything is shaking.... Stopped at last, we grab the tail gunner and in our heavy flying leather, we jump down like stiff old men but then we are off and running with him like sprinters. The crash crew trained for their job, quickly intercept us and force us all into the ambulances and we're driven to the station sick bay. No words are spoken. Just a shot in the arm and sleep.

"Hours later I wake up to a smiling face offering a cup of tea. I have a feeling of peace and for a moment wonder whether I have died. Then reality floods back and I find out that the tail gunner will recover. He is in a Canadian Military Hospital and I'll be out of sick bay tomorrow. Another op completed. *P Popsy* will go for repairs and coming up for me.... ten glorious days of leave in London."

And so Schellin remembers his hazardous time as an air gunner with a deep sense of comradeship for the men with whom he flew, an abiding sadness for friends lost, and respect for the Luftwaffe Fighter Wing that harassed the bombers.

"They were well-disciplined professionals. We called them The Abbeyville Boys. No shooting of baled-out crews or the like."

Martin Schellin collected funds on Wings Day in 1984. The RCAF flag is one that flew over the dispersal hut, 408 Squadron, at Lincton-on-Ouse in WWII.

And there was the red-letter day when royalty called.

"During 1944, No. 6 Group RCAF flyers had been awarded so many decorations that, breaking with custom, the King and Queen and the two princesses came to Linton and made the investitures in front of our Halifaxes."

With a slightly bitter wistfulness Martin Schellin notes, "Allerton Hall has been returned to the family who owned it. The mementos are the graves in Harrowgate Churchyard. Perhaps there are still some people in Tollerton village who can remember the young guys who'd cycle out from Linton-on-Ouse, have a few pints of beer, then walk the three miles or so back to camp – not chancing to 'fly their bikes'."

The air gunner survivor of numerous ops always flies with his wartime mascot – a 1922 Canadian nickel, plus the piece of German shrapnel he found in his mid-upper turret. And when his hand pains him, he is reminded of those freezing nights he spent flying over Europe in *P Popsy.*

Editor's note: By the end of 1944, 87% of No. 6 Group, Bomber Command was Canadianized. From its formation in 1942, and VE Day it suffered 4272 fatal operational casualties to Canadian personnel. The Group flew 40,822 sorties with 814 aircraft lost on ops. Many other Canadians were still serving in RAF squadrons. Ground crew strength was 93% at the end of 1944, plus 509 members RCAF WD. In Bomber Command alone at war's end the RCAF had close to 1250 pilots, 1300 navigators, 1000 air bombers, 1600 air gunners and 750 wireless operators – excluding Canadians in No. 6 RCAF Group. *Arms, Men, and Governments* by C.P. Stacey.

Since 1946 **Martin Schellin** has been employed by the Overseas Corporation of General Motors Ltd. He and his wife, Joyce, live near Dunstable in England.

27

RCAF (Women's Division)

One of the First

In October 1941, the first 150 candidates were chosen for service with the RCAF (Women's Division) and **Margaret McClelland** from Saskatchewan had the distinction of being among them.

Section Officer Margaret McClelland was stationed in Brandon, Manitoba, in 1942.

SHE RECALLS THAT she was summoned to Saskatoon for an interview. "I was surprised to see eighty women gathered there. What an odd mix we were. And all on time for the appointment! Only six of us were selected."

Margaret was one of a trio of teachers on the High School staff at Gowan, Saskatchewan. During a single week the war effort would take all three.

"It was a Wednesday morning when the other woman teacher received a letter advising her to report to the Munitions Inspection Board. That same afternoon a telegram arrived for the principal. He was off the join the RCAF. My notice came the next morning and the full wrath of the harassed School Board descended on me. But the following Monday I was gone too, on my way to the Manning Depot, Toronto, formerly the Havergal Ladies College.

"We slept in two large dormitories, sixty plus in ours on the second floor. One morning the RCAF bugler encountered a nude WD rushing to the bathroom. He never came past the first floor after that.

"Although it was several weeks before we were issued uniforms, we were being drilled unmercifully by a big, red-headed RCAF sergeant-major. He seemed utterly disgusted with his assignment of turning a bunch of women into a squad that knew its left foot from its right. He barked and bellowed while we cowered and stamped. Slated for church parade one sunny Sunday morning, we were milling about in our best civilian finery, when sarge called for the marker. A tall girl in a big floppy hat stepped forth smartly, her hat undulating at every pace. That broke 'sarge' up completely and from then on we were on a much better footing.

"Time came for fifty commissions to be handed out and a lot of us were sure that they'd been given to women from wealthy and/or politically-connected families. I was idealist then and felt devasted.

"More recruits were arriving and meanwhile it was what to do with 100 corporals. As one of them I worked in the post office, used up sugar rations making fudge in the kitchen, and acted as recording clerk at inoculation parade. Fifty of us went to the Margaret Eaton School and took a month-long calisthenics course. This consisted of an hour lectures, and four

226

hours on the floor performing calisthenics, games, rhythmics, and folk dancing. At the same time we were spending two hours a day on the parade square being transformed into a crack drill squad. By the end of that month we were certainly much fitter – but only two of us were not bandaged or hurting somewhere.

"In the spring of 1942, 150 WDs, 2 corporals, 1 sergeant and two officers were posted to Claresholm, Alberta. The other corporal and I guarded the two railcars full of girls with our lives – at times even locking the doors.

"The men on the station were totally confused by our strange uniforms and flat hats and at first saluted everyone

CWAC Ambulance drivers awaiting departure of a repatriation convoy, Farnorough, Hants., England, 12 January 1945. (left to right) Privates Mina Bray, Elda Austin, Olive Baguley, Mary Mclennan, Elfreda Duggan, Roonie Sigurdson, and Gladys Deneau.

wearing a skirt. And joy, those many years ago. They'd even apologize to us if we happened to overhear them swearing.

"When a plane crashed into a barracks we remembered and obeyed the strict instructions not to run to the scene of a crash. We were the only ones on the station who paid heed to those orders.

"I'd just finished one particularly long day of hard work and remember arriving back at the block near midnight. The spring weather was cold and raw. My legs were raw too, where my four-buckle glamour boots rubbed them. I managed to get a bath and with only four tubs among 150 women, a soaking was a rare treat. I sat in the tub thinking that my mother had certainly been right when she warned me that there'd be days like the one I'd just been through.

"In May 1942, I was commissioned and sent to Brandon as a Messing Officer. I hated it. I had a head cook who hid bags of flour and sugar in the attic of the Mess, disliked me intensely but for some reason I never knew, he once defended my honour and lost a front tooth in the process. Just prior to leaving that job I had to cope with training a nervous replacement, the agony of a severe sore throat, and an official visit from Princess Alice. Her standard kept falling off the limousine and as the chauffeur got out to fix it yet again, her suggestion, loud and clear was 'Just spit on it, drivah, just spit on it!'"

Section Officer Margaret McClelland was much happier when she was posted back to Administration duties.

She remained in the RCAF until March 1945 and then resumed a teaching career. The first post-war job she took was in connection with the Canadian Veterans Training Plan when she worked in Saskatoon.

Margaret (McClelland) Barclay lives in Regina, Saskatchewan.

28

Sand and Flies and Spitfires

Clifford L. Macdonald grew up in Springhill, a village in the Eastern Townships of Quebec. He enlisted in the RCAF almost exactly a century after his ancestors had arrived in the region from the Isle of Lewis. Sergeant Clifford Macdonald (on the right) and 417 Squadron friends encamped at Tripoli, Libya in 1943.

W HY HAD HE volunteered in 1940?

"For the country. And I badly wanted to fly. When they told me that at twenty-nine, I was too old to train for air crew, I signed on for ground duties."

He and Oriel Selby were married while he was on embarkation leave in January 1942. Then came brief stops in Ireland and England, and two weeks at Tain in Scotland "where the cattle grow long hair to keep warm in summer" and where he joined RCAF Squadron No. 417.

Aboard ship, with a uniform change to tropical gear, the men of 417 Squadron sailed the long way round to North Africa, spending a week in Durban en route. The Axis powers controlled the Mediterranean and the unit arrived in Suez ready to take its part in battle actions designed to change that situation.

Although his later experiences in Malta, Sicily and Italy were equally arduous and risky, Cliff Macdonald's verbal flash-backs most often refer to his period of war service in North Africa. Like desert sand, the memories sweep over him with little or no warning.

The dysentery 'bug' was there to greet him almost as soon as he set foot in the Port of Suez. Soon any leave lasting longer than forty-eight hours became a memory. Even had the Presbyterian-raised sergeant been so inclined, the legendary 'fleshpots' of Cairo, Rome and Paris were well out of his reach.

"A group of us had been all set for a quick trip to Jerusalem by truck but that was cancelled out by the Battle of El Alemein. Orders sent us off in the opposite direction.

"Before our own planes arrived we lent a hand to the Americans who were flying B25s, twin-engined Mitchell bombers which at that time, had no armament. I was up testing with them one day when the bloody fools deliberately flew over the front lines and drew ack-ack fire. It was a relief when the pilot turned round with 'Time to go back. The smell's getting stronger. We must be close to Cairo.' Fliers swore that the pollution from Cairo was identifiable from the air some fifty miles away.

"The Squadron flew Hurricanes at first and then the beautiful planes, Spitfires. Officially I worked in Stores but out there we interchanged jobs to some extent so I inspected planes and did various other chores."

RCAF Squadron 417, two RAF Squadrons, one Australian and one South African squadron constituted a Wing under the command of Canadian veteran ace pilot, Stan "The Bull" Turner.

"Initially we flew protection for the Port of Suez where the squadron bagged its first enemy aircraft, a JU 88 shot down by Flt/Sgt J.H.G. Laguerrier of Montreal. Then it was up to Alexandria with its lovely miles-long beaches of white sand, and eastward again to Rosetta. Once the Eighth Army began their Gazala Gallop we flew close support. Advance, retreat, advance along the North African coast. Our temporary 'dromes consisted of not much more than portable corrugated iron runways, wide enough to take our planes and about thirty feet long. An army engineering section would take them up, transport them to the next 'station' and set then down again. And so it went on. If in an advance party, we didn't stop long enough to pitch tents. We just slept under our trucks. One good thing about the desert, it cooled off enough at night to allow sleep. Quite apart from being in the battle zone, we would have found 1942 extraordinary for we saw no clouds in the sky from May until September.

"The other squadrons dubbed us The Crazy Canadians, mainly because we insisted on working on through the three-hour-long siesta. They'd rest. We figured we were out there to win the war so what the heck, we might as well get on with the job. When the army was in the thick of things, our planes would go up on strafing and light bombing missions as often as five times a day.

"On one of our frequent moves we got a flat near El Daba. Someone in the back of the truck dropped the spare out and to our alarm, it bounced and rolled its way into the middle of a minefield. We had to have that tire and there was nothing else for it — two of us followed very carefully in the big tire's tracks and then rolled it back just as carefuly in those exact same tracks. We were both a bit shaky at the end of it.

"All you could do when caught in a sandstorm was to cover up everything possibe and wait until it blew itself out. It seemed that sand could penetrate anywhere, even lodging itself between your teeth. No doubt there is some in my old kit bag yet.

"Natives in the cities would suddenly lie down on the sidewalks and take naps. Shoeshine fellas dogged us and were damned nuisances. You'd no sooner had your shoes cleaned when a few yards further on, you'd be pestered again with 'shoeshine, shoeshine' from a chorus likely to include the fella you'd just paid. The occasional one would brazenly spill stuff on your shoes. Some of us watched one fella trying the old second-go-round with two Aussies walking ahead of us. One Aussie allowed the chap to shine his shoes again, then hoisted him up on a picket fence and left him there – dangling by his burnoose. As we went by he was kicking and yelling and spitting in fury.

"The official beer ration was one bottle per two men per week, (perhaps). There was wry amusement on both sides when we Canadians were issued with Scotch beer and the RAF boys got our Canadian ale. The other nationalities envied our ability to obtain and pay for larger quantities from the NAAFI (Navy, Army and Air Force Institute). To their one case of forty-eight bottles, we might come back with ten cases. And the natives would shake their heads and repeat 'crazeee Canadians'. When the squadron held a party in the sands of Egypt to celebrate the first anniversary of 417's formation, we went through twenty-two cases by next morning. Not a bottle left. We were working a steady and full nine days out of every ten so life out there was certainly not all beer and skittles.

"Flies were like the sand. Everywhere. Natives seemed to ignore the flies settled around nose, eyes and mouth. In contrast, we'd keep waving our hands about in vain attempts to disperse them. Bread was bought locally and at first we sat trying to pick out the flies that were baked into it. A tiresome job and we soon buttered the bread and ate flies and all.

"At least they hadn't contaminated the inside of tangerines we'd buy from a native vendor who came around chanting 'Tangerines made in Palestine (pronounced Palesteen). Good for the stomach.' Hardtack and bully beef were our staples. For one four-week period we ate hardtack and bully for breakfast, dinner and supper.

"Our CO was Squadron Leader Bert 'Hardtack' Houle from Northern Ontario. After our Spits landed one day,

232

The 417 Squadron Spitfires share runways with sheep near Naples, Italy in 1944.

another pilot told me that he'd been flying tailgate to 'Hard-tack' when they'd spotted a Jerry, 'You guys stay up there and watch how it's done' came the leader's terse command as he peeled off in pursuit. The lesson was recorded on camera and I managed to scrounge a picture of the enemy plane plunging earthward.

"Squadron Leader Houle earned a DSO and a DFC and Bar. He told us later about a policeman in Canada who doubted that he was old enough to have earned the decorations. Phoney war heroes were about the land and Bert Houle did not take kindly to such remarks. The crack pilot was also a pretty fair wrestler and the cop reaped his reward for the insinuation, a broken arm.

"It was January 1943, and we'd covered 1500 miles since El Alemein as we rolled into Tripoli on the heels of New Zealand troops. That same morning Jerry had pulled out in a hurry and the Kiwis came on a stash of good wine in barrels that hadn't

Clifford MacDonald (on the right) and friends encamped at Tripoli, Libya in 1943.

been bullet-holed. The campaign had been going well and here was a chance to celebrate. The result was a binge. It was pay parade time but in the circumstances the Adjutant, Flight-Lieutenant James Sinclair (later a minister in the Pearson government) refused to pay us. Our popular and respected adjutant, known to all as Jim or Jimmy, paid us after we'd slept it off. He and several other officers had sampled and approved the wine for themselves.

"Although I watched endlessly long columns of Italian and German prisoners walking their way to captivity, I had contact with only one. He was a German newsman and we confiscated his camera. On development of the film, one picture showed none other than General Erwin Rommel drinking a toast. 'To the victory of Egypt' our prisoner explained loyally. I scrounged a copy of that one, too.

"I was to have a chance encounter with Rommel's opposite number, our own General Bernard Montgomery. We were an advance party in convoy on our way to yet another landing field. Halted by the roadside near Halfaya (Hellfire) Pass, we were brewing up when this Jeep came along, stopped, and there he was, black beret and all, and coming towards us. He chatted for a few minutes about the way the advance was going. Discretion prevented us from offering him tea. For one thing he was a general and for another we were using high octane fuel for the brew up. Monty, the renowned abstainer, surprised us by pulling a pack of cigarettes from his pocket and offering them around. Then we all saluted and he drove on.

"Holding our mugs of tea, we discussed the moment and the man, and drew on the Players Medium cigarettes just received at *HIS* own hand. It had been one of those unexpected fleeting experiences of wartime. Too bad, I didn't get a picture!".

In January 1945, Sergeant **C.L. Macdonald** left Italy for Britain and from thence it was home to Canada and demobilization. He resumed his work in the textile industry and now retired, he lives with his wife Oriel, in Brantford, Ontario.

29

Beating the Odds

Pilot Officer Earle White of RAF Squadron 58, based at Linton-on-Ouse, Yorkshire, in October 1941.

D̲r̲. ᴇᴀʀʟᴇ ᴀ. ᴡʜɪᴛᴇ is a retired ʀᴄᴀꜰ flier who experienced one hair-raising situation after another during World War II. Possessed of indomitable spirit and remarkable fortitude, he somehow survived the hardships inflicted on his mind and body. "I joined the ʀᴄᴀꜰ immediately after graduating from McGill University with BA (pre-med and high school teacher's diploma) and began air crew training on 5 September 1940. Before being commissioned in May 1941, I trained as observer (navigation and bomb aimer) at Malton, and Jarvis, Ontario and Rivers, Manitoba.

"A month later I boarded the *California*, an armed merchant cruiser sailing in convoy for Britain but due to heavy U boat activity, some 150 of us were dumped off in Iceland for a couple of weeks. About half were Australians who'd trained in Canada; approximately ten per cent of us commissioned, the rest sergeants. We left Iceland in steel-hulled British fishing boats and our escort to Gourock, Scotland was the battleship *Prince of Wales*, doomed to be sunk by the Japanese that December."

In July 1941, Pilot Officer E.A. White of Mansonville, Quebec was taking operational training on Whitley bombers at Abingdon, Berkshire. Posting to 58 Squadron at Linton-on-Ouse, Yorkshire came in August.

The target for his first operational raid was the docks at Ostend and as he quipped to a reporter afterwards, he was 'on his toes in more ways than one'. Being navigator-bomb aimer on the flight, he was at the ready, kneeling over the bomb hatch when inadvertedly his toe caught on the catch – the door gave way beneath him – and he fell three-quarters of the way out of the plane!

"We were on our final bomb run and I was giving directions to pilot. Right ... right ... steady ... with accompanying body English, no doubt. When the bomb hatch opened I wasn't thinking bomb accuracy or anything else. Both arms instinctively wrapped themselves around the bomb sight, the trigger on the 'tit' was squeezed and the bombs went. The irony was that the automatic cameras recorded a direct hit and that helped make the episode newsworthy. I couldn't even bring up my microphone to talk. The second pilot checked to see what was going on, and New Zealand pilot, P/O Manders, swung

Earle White had gunnery practice in this type of Fairey Battle trainer in Jarvis, Ontario in March 1941.

out to sea. He lowered flaps to reduce speed and force of slipstream while the second pilot came down to help me pull back into the plane. Fortunately no enemy planes were after us."

The buffetting on the fuselage and strain on his muscles left him painfully stiff and bruised for days. He was ribbed unmercifully by squadron members and had to pay the maximum one pound fine for line-shooting and getting his name in the papers. His own sense of humour prompts him to describe his first op ordeal as "just preliminary training for my final op."

Flight Lieutenant (F/Lt) E.A. White, continues the story to tell of more truly incredible experiences from his war years.

"By April 1942, all Whitleys had been retired from ops over Germany and my squadron was posted to Coastal Command. Because experienced Canadians were at a premium and 6 Group RCAF was due to replace 4 Group RAF in the Yorkshire area, I was asked to stay behind. Owing to a delay in the formation of 6 Group (where I was to take over the ground job as Station Navigation Officer) I was posted to 76 Sqdn, Middleton St. George, flying Halifax Mark II.

"On 20 June 1942, we were on our way to bomb Emden in a brand new Halifax, delivered that same day. Our own had been badly holed with one engine out on the previous night, and was unserviceable. We knew that the new plane had not been properly air-tested and our crew had taken off 'under protest'. Unable to reach altitude over 18,000 feet (6000 metres) by the time we crossed the Frisian Islands we were well behind schedule and straggling. We'd held a quick conference as to whether we should abort and return to base, deciding that Emden was an easy target and we'd earn credit for another mission.

"Unknown to us, the enemy had an ack-ack gunnery school on Terschelling. The Germans told me later that they had plotted us as a classic exercise, and since we were all alone and not taking evasive action, it was easy. Searchlights were kept off so as to give us no warning. Close to midnight we took a direct hit and the shell set the plane afire. I just had time to grab my parachute and snap it on when in a matter of a few seconds the Halifax exploded. We had 12,000 pounds of high explosives on board and petrol tanks were more than half full.

"I shall never know exactly what happened to me for I recall nothing until I was on the ground. Since I was in the nose of the plane, I believe that the force of the explosion must have blown me through the perspex. Perhaps the 'chute ring caught as I went through or perhaps I subconciously pulled it. In any event I floated down from 18,000 feet unconcious, blown out of my boots, and somewhat singed. I had a fractured skull and concussion, a few broken ribs, and shrapnel fragments in my left leg. Only three parts of the plane were found; some of the tail assembly, one engine nacelle, and a section of the pilot's cockpit with the dead pilot still in it. I was the lone survivor.

"The Germans were evidently intrigued. They told me that they'd found my 'chute which I'd attempted to bury, then picked me up 16 km away in my stockinged feet, bleeding and trying to escape. I have flashes of memory, the first being of something like a bee buzzing past my head about eight or nine in the morning. Two German soldiers saw me and fired over my head because I didn't halt on command. My next flash is of being in their barracks where they'd poured iodine on my leg and were digging bits of shrapnel out with a penknife. I found out that this was near Groningen, Holland. I am not surprised that I'd been trying to get away as it had been drilled into us that if we were shot down we should get out of the area of search (normally about a fifteen mile / 24 km radius) and hide up. Of one thing I am convinced, my subconcious was working overtime.

"I was never hospitalized but taken to Gestapo headquarters in Amsterdam where I regained my memory in a stone-walled underground cell with constantly dripping water. I am unclear as to how long I was a guest of the Gestapo but it was long enough for my family to receive a second telegram (first one 'missing in action', second one 'presumed dead'). Likely it was four to six weeks.

"One day the local gauleiter came for me and I was taken out in an enormous open car with the chauffeur separated by a glass partition and an outsize swastika flag flying from the front bumper. Sitting between the gauleiter and a high ranking German officer, I was paraded through the streets to show the locals that one of the 'Terrorfliegers' had been caught.

"Because of my concussion, it was some time before I could be interrogated. During that period they put one-inch tape on my chest to support the broken ribs; the sole medical attention I received. I wasn't physically mistreated in any way. Only psychologically. They seemed to think I spoke German but except for a few words, I did not. I was eventually taken to an interrogation centre at Frankfort-am-Mainz (Dulag Luft) where I underwent further questioning. For roughly a week I was given a range of treatment – from the so-called Red Cross

Canadian POW Dog-Tag. The German POW Dog-Tag had to be worn at all times. Flight Lieutenant Earle White became Number 301 when he was admitted to Stalag Luft III at Sagnan near Breslau in Silesia. In case of 'accident', one part was for the German records and the other to be buried with the prisoner of war.

Prisoners of war Schubin, Poland early in 1943 (left to right) were Ted Collins, England; Keith Pearce, Australia; Bill Shiells, England; Earle White, Canada; and M. Wilding, England.

representative requesting that I fill out forms so that 'my loved ones' could be notified that I was safe, to the rough guy who'd come in, slap his pistol on the table, declaring that they'd wasted enough time on me and now I was going to *talk*, to the friendly one who'd offer cigarettes and food, apologizing for the tough guy etc. etc. The friendly one told me that he'd been a waiter in the Hoffbrau, a popular restaurant and beer garden in pre-war Montreal and heavily patronized by McGill students. They knew I'd know the place.

"Surprisingly, they knew a lot about me. 'You had a good run, didn't you. We've been waiting a long time for you'. They actually knew how many ops I'd completed, which squadrons I'd been with, and my COs' names. They even showed me a photo of the squadron taken only a couple of months previously. Recognize these men? they asked. They watched my reactions to their questions and although I gave them no information then, I admit now that theirs was accurate.

"In late August or early September I became POW No. 301 at Stalag Luft III at Sagan in Silesia, Poland. A few weeks later I was one of a group 'purged' to Schubin, a camp between Poznan and Lublin.

"Previously occupied by French POWs, the long barn-like barracks block was brick-floored and filthy. We made compartments by partitioning off small areas for eight to ten men; furniture consisted of two-tiered wooden bunks with bug-infested mattresses, and tall lockers. At the end of each block were cold, cement-floored wash-houses. The communal lavatory, a foul-smelling black wooden shed with thirty-six wooden seats set above a crawling pit, was situated close to our bare earth recreation area.

"Suicide attempts were frequent but rarely successful for it took too long to bleed to death after cutting the wrist with a safety razor blade. Two successful attempts were made that fall. One man jumped from a top window of the only high building (used as a sick bay) and hit the concrete steps below. A young RAF officer calmly walked from his barrack block smoking a cigarette, and climbed the inner wire fence. He was shot in the stomach and as he lay moaning in front of the outer wire, the gathering crowd of prisoners was held back at gunpoint and prevented from going to his aid. It came close to mass mutiny when a German NCO casually rolled the dying man over with the tip of his jackboot. The airman died that same day.

"Food was scarce and a wandering cat was killed with a well-aimed stone. As we tried to retrieve the frozen carcass from between the two wire fences, the Germans played a game of firing down the line whenever anyone leaned across. After three days they relented and allowed us to salvage the cat. It made a fine stew.

"The winter of 1942-3 was grim. Several tunnels were begun and thirty-three officers escaped although almost all were recaptured. The Germans reported to us that two of them, Lt. Commander James Buckley RN (Fleet Air Arm) and Flying Officer (F/O) Thompson, were drowned as they attempted to cross the Skagerrak in a small boat.

"An adjacent camp housed Russian survivors of Sebastopol, about two hundred of them at time of our arrival. The German Camp Commandant told us with sadistic pleasure about conditions there, including the fact that in their desperate situation, some had resorted to eating their dead. Since the Russians had no Red Cross they had only German rations. We received permission to send over a small consignment of food and bits of clothing. In return the senior Russian officer wrote thanking

242

us and said that they were suffering daily loss of life. There were only seventy-three of them surviving.

"By April 1943, we were returned to Stalag Luft III and the tender care of the Luftwaffe. Many books have been written about life there. In the main life was monotonous. We shuffled around the sand circuit day after day, often disposing of tunnelling sand from two bags (usually made from the legs and arms of heavy underwear) hung around our waists, the trickle being controlled by drawstings. We were wearing long Polish greatcoats and this method of disposal was never discovered.

"American, Canadian and British Red Cross parcels were our ticket to survival. Our mainstay. The object was to provide one ten-pound parcel per prisoner per week. This ratio was never reached but sometimes there was one parcel to two men and more often, one parcel between four. We were deprived of Red Cross parcels for a ten week period in the spring of '43 but this was not gratuitous cruelty. The Germans were very short on supplies themselves; there were no Red Cross parcels in the stores and they had nothing but bare rations to give us. Their rations called for one hot meal per day, plus vegetables in season, bread (50% sawdust by later analysis), and sometimes small amounts of sugar and jam. During that ten weeks we ate rotten potatoes and sawdust bread and ended up having to be counted in our beds, so many were too weak to stand outside. The hot meal was a weak soup or stew containing bits of turnip or cabbage or barley, and very rarely bits of meat. My meat portion one day, consisted of a dog's paw with hair still on it.

"The influx of captured American airmen became so great that compounds had to be added to house approximately 10,000 Air Force officers. During 1944, I was passed for repatriation as a 'Grand Blessé' to be exchanged for German wounded. Basically an American exchange, only two of us from the East compound were to go, most of the Americans being in the Centre block. After making my application, I was taken to a hospital in Czechoslovakia for examination. On the return trip we changed trains at Goerlitz and while there a German civilian told my guard about some escaped prisoners of war being held in the local police station. We found out later that it was from Goerlitz that fifty escapees from Luft III were taken out in twos and threes and cold-bloodedly shot. And at this time the Germans posted notices around the camp

243

announcing that escaping was no longer a sport – anyone attempting it would be shot. Along with the other fellow in our compound, an American in the RAF, I was left behind when the U.S. repatriates left. It triggered a particularly depressing period for me.

"Medical facilities were almost non-existent at Stalag Luft III, just a small sick bay in the Vorlager with one British doctor to all five compounds. The Vorlaeger was an area enclosed by barbed wire but without the machine-gun towers. It housed German administration offices, stores, showers and also the sick bay, solitary detention cells, and a small compound of Russian slave workers. Standard treatment for a broken limb was a splint and an aspirin. Should more entensive care be deemed necessary, the patient was sent away but this was rare – except for violent cases who'd 'gone around the bend'. And those were not uncommon.

"A German officer at Luft III, Hauptmann (Captain) Pieber, was so sickened by the murder of the fifty airmen by the Gestapo that he became our ally. He warned us well in advance that we were likely to be moved out at short notice and that we should prepare. Most of us managed to sew braces to a kit bag, and packed a towel and Red Cross woollen socks. My closest friend, the late Mel Gifford of Sherbrooke, Quebec, and I built a sled of sorts by nailing a box on a couple of runners carved from bed boards. It would last us about a week.

"On a late January evening our orders came to leave. They permitted us to raid the Red Cross stores and take a food parcel each. We threw the heavier tins over the fence to the still-confined Russian POWs.

"And so, at -30 degrees Fahrenheit the forced march began. Slowly, under the ruthless supervison of SS troops, our long shabby column with its thousands of Allied air force officers, moved out.

"The next day we met a very long column of Russian POWs heading for Luft III, according to Pieber. (In 1957, I clipped an item from the Winnipeg Free Press stating that a mass grave containing thousands of bodies had been uncovered at Stalag Luft III, presumably that was the fate of those Russian POWs). On the second night we halted and were crowded into a

244

school. When we were not walking all night we were usually shepherded hurriedly into a church or school. Five days after setting out we received our first food from the guards, half a loaf of black bread each. Our preparations had paid off. More recent arrivals among the Americans had scoffed when we'd passed on Pieber's warning. 'Aw, they wouldn't do that to us' type of comment — and they suffered badly. Our ragged column passed through many small towns; in one the street was lined with women and many of them cried as we staggered by. One brought a pail of water and I saw an SS guard use his rifle with bayonet to topple her and her water over the snowbank.

"One night several hundred of us were put in a large barn for the night. Mel and I clambered down to a lower level among the cows and after milking one into a tin can, we slept between two of them. We'd drunk our first fresh milk in nearly three years and I can still remember the wonderful taste! Next morning we traded cigarettes for hot water at the farmhouse. Our guards gave permission and likely took their cut for the Germans were rationed to two cigarettes a day.

"The road became obstructed by Ost Volk, Germans who'd been living in Poland and were fleeing the Russians. They'd just made it across the last remaining bridge over the Oder which would be closed later in the day. I remember giving a package of cigarettes to a young mother with two little children in a rickety sleigh pulled by a starving horse. One child had frozen to death and I hoped the mother would be able to barter the cigarettes to help save the other one. The refugee column was miles long. Women and children and a few very old men.

"Memories crowd in from the first march I passing a siding with its rows of miniature railway cars each containing a painted face at the window. The faces belonged to girls from concentration camps and forced into prostitution as 'feldhores' ... Russian cavalry moving through us with the option of fighting for the Germans against their own or being shot ... an Italian battalion reluctantly moving up and willing to trade ground sheets for a couple of cigarettes. I bought a water canteen for one cigarette and a chicken for two.

"Our next stop was at Muskau just inside the German

border where we were herded into the coal shed of a bomb-damaged glass factory. I think we'd been on the march about two weeks then and never out of our clothes. Mel and I and a few others decided that we didn't care for the coal dump and succeeded in getting into the factory itself where it felt lovely and warm. We climbed on to the conveyor belt and went to sleep. Hauptmann Pieber found us and warned that if the belt was started up we'd go right into the ovens. The blessed warmth persuaded us to take the chance. We stayed put that night and all next day.

"In the evening 2000 of us were counted off and once again marched out into the night. Mel's knee was the size of a football and I had to leave without him. He was eventually liberated by the Russians but didn't get back to England until June. Consequently, I'd have to find another best man for my marriage to my English fiancee at Boston, Lincolnshire on 30 May.

"We walked all night and as the weather turned milder, the road became slush and very difficult. Next day we stopped in a large barracks and were told that we'd be staying. It was warm in there and I made the mistake of taking off my boots. About 3 p.m. they told us that we'd be moving on. No way could I get my boots back on my swollen feet. By this time there were fewer than 1800 left of the original 2000 prisoners.

"In stockinged feet I struggled on as best I could through the slush and snow. Relief came that evening when we were put in cattle cars and transported to Marlag O camp near Bremen. It was fortunate for me that the walking ordeal was over, at least temporarily. For the last kilometre or two I'd been down on my knees and needed help from two comrades. Bits of woollen socks were embedded in my painful raw feet and it was weeks before I could walk comfortably again.

"We stayed at Marlag O until April when we moved off again. This time the weather was pleasant and we were guarded by old marine guards from the First War. They permitted us to go at our own speed and even helped us to steal eggs, bicycles, etc. The Germans had very nice baby carriages and one of our boys traded two cigarettes and a small amount of Nescafe for one. The mother hiked her baby on to her shoulder while he piled his own and other POWs belongings into the carriage and pushed off.

"Personal parcels from Canada, sent through the Red Cross, were allowed from relatives and usually took about a year in transit. I received two from home during my near three years as a prisoner. Cigarettes however, were sent in abundance and direct from the factory. My sister sent 1000 each month at a cost of $1.69. When we left Stalag Luft III, Mel Gifford and I had stockpiled around 50,000 cigarettes. We each carried over 2000 on the march, rather than the heavier food. We knew that if need be, we'd be able to trade cigarettes for food. Later on, cigarettes became relatively scarce and were sold and traded among us on a rough scale of $100 per 100 cigarettes.

"We came across a newly-built village for children and in it there were thousands of war orphans and bombing victims from all over Germany. Kids came offering bunches of flowers when we stopped for lunch by the roadside. I had a packet of raisins and a circle of little girls (five or six years old) sang for us and I gave them one raisin each. An older girl, perhaps ten, with a steel brace on her leg, had stood watching. I called her over and gave her a small piece of chocolate from an American D bar. Her eyes lit up and she curtsied prettily with her danke schon. About a mile down the road we stopped again and the same little girl came limping up and stood close by. I just had to give her another little nub of chocolate.

"This march was comparatively pleasant. We slept on the ground and only two of our group were shot to death by a guard. In that guard's case, his family had recently been wiped out by bombing. One day we were strafed by one of our own planes and one night we were bombed by another. No casualties. We crossed the Elbe above Hamburg and that night it rained, and having caught a cold, I didn't appreciate sleeping in the mud. Next day the Germans offered to put us on trucks. I expected numerous volunteers but there were only a few of us. The rest thought there was safety in numbers and they may have been right. They were liberated and back in England long before I was.

"I ended the war in a French POW camp at Lubeck on the Baltic. I'd arrived there by train in a covered cattle car with about a dozen other air force officers and two armed guards. A

Pilot Officer Earle White and Radar Operator Winifred Woods ATS of Boston, Lincolnshire, England soon after their marriage in May 1945. Later, in 1955 Win Woods won a two week, all expenses honeymoon for them in Hawaii by placing first in a *Liberty* magazine writing contest called "Chance Meeting".

number of high ranking concentration camp evacuees (from Sachsenhausen I believe) were in open cattle cars divided by barbed wire with mounted machine-guns at one end. For them it was standing room only on the other side of the wire. I was very frightened on that train but luckily it was a short trip from Hamburg to Lubeck. We understood that the Germans were planning to take political prisoners to Norway for use in negotiations. At Lubeck they were put aboard barges and we were taken to the French camp. The barges were sunk during an RAF raid on the harbour and all those political prisoners drowned.

"British forces liberated us in early May and I was taken to a German aerodrome near Lunenburg to be flown to England. Unfortunately it was a fighter 'drome and bombers could not land. It was there, as senior officer of our group, that I met with the Swiss representative. The Swiss were our protecting power. He informed me about the drownings at Lubeck, and told me another interesting item. The Swiss said he was in Germany to investigate a rumour. After the fire-bombing of Dresden, Hitler ordered that for every person killed in Dresden, an Allied prisoner of war was to be shot – starting with the airmen in Stalag Luft III. He signed the order and passed it on to Himmler for execution but for reasons unknown, Himmler had the order stopped. The Swiss had verified this and his only

248

conjecture was that, because the war was so obviously nearing its end, Himmler may have gambled on the cancellation being in his favour later.

"While at Lunenburg three of us volunteered to go with a medical team to the nearby Belsen concentration camp. The first thing I did was to puke my guts out. Many of the inmates, though still alive, were too weak and ill to be moved anywhere. I can only say that things were terrible there; even now, I find it very hard to think about what I saw. For three days we did what little we could to help.

"By mid-May 1945, I was back in England, weighing in at 115 pounds."

On his return to Canada, F/Lt. **Earle A. White** was awarded a 70% disability pension. He went back to McGill University and graduated in dentistry in 1950. With his wife Winifred, Dr. E.A. White now resides in Summerland, British Columbia.

30

Greenland Ordeal

Based at Dorval, Quebec, the fledgling Atlantic Ferry Organization grew rapidly after its founding in 1940; by the war's end 9000 aircraft had been delivered to various theatres of combat. Its official title had evolved to No. 45 Group, Transport Command, RAF, in 1943 – but the shorter and more romantic *Ferry Command* was the name that stuck. **Robert E. Coffman, Norman E. Greenaway and Ronald E. Snow** were three airmen of that command who had a miraculous escape. Ronald Snow, Radio Officer with the Ferry Command Organization was photographed in Montreal in 1941.

By OCTOBER 1943, aging Hampden twin-engined bombers were being replaced in the war zones by newer and more efficient aircraft. Hampden AE 309 was on its way from England to Patricia Bay, British Columbia and once there, it would be used for training purposes.

Robert Coffman, an American from Baton Rouge was pilot and captain of its three-man crew. Coffman's maturity and several years experience as a civil airline pilot would soon prove invaluable.

Twenty-three year old Flying Officer Norman Greenaway RCAF, was the navigator. Prior to enlisting, Ted Greenaway had worked in the hardrock mines of British Columbia. On graduation from RCAF Observers School, the Camrose, Alberta native had been posted to RAF Ferry Command at Dorval.

Ronald Snow, a twenty-two year old from Digby, Nova Scotia was the radio officer. He had graduated from the Marconi Radio School in Halifax and signed with the Canadian Merchant Navy in January 1941. After a few voyages he heard that radio operators were needed as crew to ferry hot-off-the-assembly-line bombers across the Atlantic. He applied and was accepted by the Atlantic Ferry Organization.

Thrown together by a chance of war, the three men melded into a compatible and efficient team.

On this, their second trip across the hazardous northern route with a Hampden, the flight from Scotland to Iceland had been without incident. Following a delay because of weather, the plane had left Reykjavik at 1000 hrs on 14 October 1943. It was scheduled to call at Bluie West One in Greenland, Goose Bay, and Dorval where another crew would take over and fly the aircraft to British Columbia.

At 1310 hrs and flying at 9000 feet (3000 metres), they were off the east coast of Greenland when without warning, the port engine suddenly stopped dead. Because the Hampden was equipped with non-feathering propellers it was impossible for Captain Coffman to maintain altitude. So he concentrated on keeping the plane steady while flying on one engine and gradually losing height.

Radio Officer Snow tried to send SOS signals but the power generator running the radio had already failed when the port engine gave out. In any case, they were in skip distance, a zone where signals could not penetrate the atmosphere.

For an hour the pilot skilfully manoeuvred the crippled plane but then, at 4500 feet, it went into a tight spin. Down and down, round and round out of control until at about 1000 feet – miraculously it seemed – Coffman managed to get it straightened out. He headed it toward the Greenland coast. Greenland, called by some fliers 'the asshole of the Arctic' was an estimated fifteen miles away.

Ron Snow observed "Of course there was nothing to do then but look for a clear spot to ditch. The pack ice stretched from five to ten miles from the coastline."

Aiming the plane down into a clear furrow of water that showed among the ice floes, the thirty-two year old captain completed his first ditching. His crew enthusiastically agreed that he had done a masterful job.

The official report compiled at the end of the incident by captain and crew states: ONE HOUR LATER WAS FORCED TO LAND ON THE SEA WHICH WAS SMOOTH AND CALM. UPON HIT-TING WATER AUTOMATIC DINGHY OPERATED BY IMMERSION SWITCH AND INSTALLED IN PORT ENGINE CELL, FLOATED FREE.

Wearing flying suits over uniforms, the three men quickly stepped out on to the port wing of the fast-sinking Hampden and down into the inflated rubber dinghy. With them they carried emergency supplies consisting of 12 one-pint cans of water, 1 large first aid kit, 3 small cans of concentrated food tablets, 6 bars chocolate, 1 one inch Very pistol (flare gun), 27 Very cartridges, 1 heliograph, 1 distress flag and 1 pair canvas hand paddles.

In less than two minutes after she had hit the water, Hampden AE 309 had rolled slightly and slipped beneath the surface to be swallowed up by the ocean.

At an estimated distance of ten to fifteen miles, the men could see a great spur of rock rising some 2000 feet out of the sea. Captain Coffman set the small dinghy's course in that direction and the airmen began a twenty-hour-long nightmar-ish journey through the unstable, ever-shifting ice pack. Pro-gress impeded by enormous blocks of ice, some the size of small buildings. These icebergs ground and broke against one another with terrifyingly loud cracks, roars, and rumbles.

With those frightening sounds echoing all around them, and amidst the eerie effect of the full moon reflecting on the ice, the men took turns paddling the tiny boat while picking their way between the bergs and brash ice. At other times they were forced to toss and drift with the strong coastal current.

Soaked and exhausted, they struggled on to the rocky island of Umanarsuk at mid-morning. It was necessary to drag their weary bodies and the dinghy a further 100 feet up the slope before they found a suitable ledge on which to place the craft.

As Ted Greenaway recalled, "The island was an acre or two in area – really just a pinnacle of rock a hundred yards or so off the mainland. In fact, we thought we were on the mainland when we reached it."

On 15 October the temperature ranged from 15-20 Fahrenheit. The weather was fair and it was possible to dry a few articles of lighter clothing. Morale was good and their hopes of rescue high.

"It seemed to us then," commented Ron Snow "that after surviving the trauma of spinning and ditching, we stood a good chance of getting out of there with our lives."

That same day three high-flying planes were sighted. Two were headed east and the third flew towards the north-east. The marooned men fired the Very pistol and flashed the heliograph but there was no sign that their signals were seen.

Then came their first night on Umanarsuk. Physically and mentally exhausted, they piled inside the small dinghy and attempted to sleep. Around midnight sleet began to fall and they hunted for a cave in which to shelter but the only one found proved too small. Back they went to the dinghy where common sense and expediency saw them deflate the rubber boat to a suitable extent and then curl up beneath it.

Their heavy sheepskin-lined flying boots never completely thawed or dried out and this was a major problem. Trying to prevent frostbite they would rub each other's feet and before sleeping they would place bare feet under the flying suit and against the warmth of another body.

They formulated a daily rationing plan. For each man there was to be one square of chocolate, two malted milk tablets (cut to one after three days) and a pint of water to be divided three ways. When weather permitted and strength allowed, they explored the island and in the first days found drinkable water in crevices. But the rock was entirely devoid of edible vegetation and animal life.

TWO DAYS OF CLEAR COLD WEATHER FOLLOWED THE SLEET STORM WHICH IN TURN WAS FOLLOWED BY A TERRIFIC WIND STORM WHICH BLEW SEA SPRAY SO HIGH PARTY WAS SOAKED AND FORCED TO MOVE ONE HUNDRED FEET HIGHER ON THE ROCKY SLOPE, THE SEA SPRAY TURNED ALL THE WATER ON THE ISLAND BRACKISH. THE FOLLOWING DAY A TWO-MASTED SHIP WAS SIGHTED, GOING NORTH ABOUT TEN OR FIFTEEN MILES FROM THE SHORE. SIX VERY SHOTS WERE FIRED, AND ALTHOUGH THE WEATHER AND SUN WERE UNSUITABLE FOR ITS USE AN ATTEMPT WAS MADE TO USE THE HELIOGRAPH. BUT ALL ATTEMPTS TO ATTRACT ATTENTION FAILED. THE FOLLOWING DAY WAS CLOUDY AND COLD FOL-LOWED BY A SEVERE SNOW STORM. THE CREW USED THE DINGHY FOR SHELTER THROUGHOUT THEIR STAY ON THE ISLAND. (An excerpt from the official report — *Editor*)

The men managed to obtain small amounts of extra water from underneath the dinghy where snow melted from their body heat. To draw up the precious liquid they would use the straw-like tubes meant for inflating their Mae West life-jackets.

In order to stay alert they would tell jokes and talk of childhood times. They would recount tales of places they had been and of meals they had eaten. Food they had enjoyed was a frequent topic surpassed only by talk of fantastic meals they would have when they returned to civilization.

An expedition undertaken by two of the men was described by Ron Snow. "One day Coffman and I made the long and difficult climb to the top of the rock, and jammed the flagstaff into a crevice up there. What an inspiring view we had! To the east we looked out on blue sea dotted with all those white-capped icebergs. And on the other side there was the massive Greenland ice cap stretching before us with some peaks jutting up through to 8000 feet or so."

The red and yellow distress flag flew bravely and snapped in the wind until that same wind tore and shredded it to nothingness. As an added feature to the magnificent and awesome primeval panorama, it lasted a mere twenty-four hours.

Up there on the top of Umanarsuk Coffman and Snow could see that there was no way they could reach the mainland without help. The coastal channel separating them was just too swift and treacherous.

After a week in freezing isolation their scanty rations were diminished and their signals remained unanswered. And they were also hit by the realization that planes would never notice them; all aircraft they saw were flying too high – close to 10,000 feet or higher in order to clear the ice cap peaks. Rescue would have to come from the sea.

Hope ran high when on the seventh day, they sighted a ship about ten miles out. Up went more flares but to no avail. That ship too, sailed on until out of sight.

Ron Snow told how their spirits took a downward turn after that ship disappeared over the horizon.

"We became somewhat bitter and for a short time blamed the whole world. We felt as if we were being taunted. Subsequently we decided that the end was near for us and we settled down to prepare ourselves the best we could. Personally, once I reconciled myself to dying, I felt an almost pleasant sense of relief. Yet a small nagging voice inside me persisted in questioning why we had come safely through so much, if only to die so soon afterwards."

By that time Ted Greenaway's feet were numbed by frostbite and Robert Coffman was suffering with his. They had existed through a week of hardship such as most would never know in a lifetime. First the nerve-shattering ditching exercise. Then the sea and fierce northern elements had combined to batter and exhaust their slowly starving bodies. Weaker and quieter, they spent much time on reflection and prayed together at regular intervals.

During his wartime career, Radio Officer R.E. Snow flew in many different types of aircraft including Mitchells, Bostons, Dakotas, Lancasters and PBY Flying Boats. He ferried on routes to Britain, Egypt, India, Australia and elsewhere. Following that seventh day on Umanarsuk, his mind would go over and over some earlier brushes with death.

On his third ferrying trip he had crewed on one of six Hudsons scheduled to fly from Gander, Newfoundland to Prestwick, Scotland. Weather was unusually rough on that one, and the icing problems were horrendous. Most of the planes were forced down long before making Prestwick. Snow's Hudson had to land in Northern Ireland. Another, forced down in Eire, was ordered to fly on or the crew would face internment. They chose to fly on and shortly afterwards perished when the plane crashed into a mountain.

Also there was his 1942, Ventura incident. That flight was from Newfoundland to Iceland to Prestwick. Between Goose Bay and Iceland the Ventura had unaccountably gone into a spiral and the pilot had brought it out over a valley of the

Lockheed-Vega 'Ventura', North America 'Mitchell', Consolidated 'Liberator' and Boeing 'Fortress' aircraft of the RAF Ferry Command en route to Britain from Dorval, Quebec, 13 May 1942.

Greenland ice caps not far from Umanarsuk. The valley was surrounded by smaller ice caps and cloud so Captain Merle Phoenix had had no alternative but to aim the nose straight up through the cloud. The Ventura responded and they flew at 11,000 feet again. The direction finder had been bent during the spiral and was unoperative. The gas was perilously low. Snow and the co-pilot were ordered by the captain to put on their life-jackets and parachutes and be ready to jump as soon as a ship was spotted. Fortunately bailing out became unnecessary when they reached Iceland safely. But just as they touched down the gas ran out and the engines quit. It had been a close call. Next day the Ventura was repaired and they continued on to Prestwick.

In addition Ron Snow remembered being a passenger on another flight when a bolt of lightning had hit the plane's trailing antennae. The lightning had travelled up into the bomb bay where the returning ferry crewmen were huddled together. They had managed to extinguish the fire that broke out in the floor area but not before one man had suffered burned feet.

Why indeed, had he survived so much only to face death again on a barren and frozen Arctic island?

It was 24 October and the eleventh day of their ordeal. It had begun badly. Once more and with fading hope they had tried to attract the attention of a plane. And once more they had failed. But fate had one of those dramatic changes of fortune in store for them.

Late that same morning Ron Snow crawled out from their miserable shelter beneath the dinghy. He looked seaward and found himself squinting at what appeared to be a stationary ship. He called the other two. In their weakened state were · they hallucinating or was it really a ship? Why would a ship want to stop out there?

The ship was real enough. She was the *Polar Bjorn*, a Norwegian vessel sailing under the American flag. She had stopped eight miles out to repair engine trouble. The *Polar Bjorn* was the last ship of the year to pass through those dangerous ice-bound waters.

As renewed hope of rescue took over, their resignation vanished and the three feeble and debilitated men mustered all remaining strength in a desperate, concerted attempt to contact the ship. They sent up the rest of their flares at intervals. The sun was shining brightly for the first time in days and this enabled them to use the heliograph to advantage. For three hours and more they took turns holding the mirror in benumbed, near useless fingers for short periods while sending regular flashes.

In mid-afternoon another lucky coincidence. An American army major decided to study the Greenland coast through binoculars. At first he dismissed the flashes on Umanarsuk as reflections from sunlight on ice and snow. But when he noticed a puff of smoke followed by the burst and fall of light from a Very rocket, he was convinced that the flashes were also signals.

Although an extensive air search was in progress, nobody on the *Polar Bjorn* had any information on the missing Hampden. Major Crowell consulted with the ship's Norwegian captain who suggested that the signallers might be German agents trying some ruse or other. The intrepid major decided that he was going to investigate anyway and was lowered into a small boat with three well-armed Norwegian sailors. Drawing near Umanarsuk they recognized the emaciated humans as marooned and defenceless Allied airmen.

As the rescue boat bobbed below them, each airman in turn was thrown a rope and then ordered to jump as the boat rose on the crest of a swell. Ron Snow still marvels about that jump.

"All of us landed in the middle of the boat – about a 12 foot jump. Under normal circumstances we might not have made it but in those wonderfully exhilarating moments our extreme weakness was somehow submerged and it seemed like an easy leap."

Aboard the *Polar Bjorn* it was decided to treat the frostbitten feet of Flying Officer Greenaway and Captain Coffman without delay. On the morning of 25 October, eleven days after their ordeal began, the crew of the lost Hampden were taken ashore at Cape Adelear, a United States weather reporting station (unknown to the castaways and only a few miles from their location).

Of the three men, Ted Greenaway suffered the most serious consequences. Like Robert Coffman, he was to spend several weeks in a Montreal hospital. Doctors worked diligently to save his feet while performing necessary toe amputations and skin grafting operations. Greenaway himself prefers for the most part to forget the Greenland incident, and states with matter-of-factness, "I eventually lost all of some of my toes and portions of others but I retained the balls of my feet and my balance was unaffected. My walking has been restricted but otherwise, no ill effects."

Robert Coffman's hands and feet responded to care and treatment in time.

Ronald Snow considered himself a fortunate man.

"My feet were frostbitten but with no lasting problems. I went back to delivering aircraft within a few months. My first trip was in a Lancaster with Captain Ray Leeward and we flew over Umanarsuk. It was then that I could fully appreciate why the search planes had not been able to spot us when they flew at the required height."

Extremes of hope and despair, courage and resignation, endurance and effort, were human emotions and disciplines that had been their weather-vanes in the eleven days of peril. Ron Snow has always thought the main results of the traumatic time were positive.

"We'd learned to respect one another and our earlier friendship was certainly solidified. And we'd realized that the Almighty had been with us throughout the ordeal."

Editor's Note: In March 1943, when No. 45 Group, Transport Command, RAF, took over the Ferry Command organization at Dorval, the operational aircrew strength had grown to 569 personnel. 279 of these were members of the RCAF, the remainder civilians and RAF.

The regular aircrews were supplemented by aircrews destined for postings overseas. Graduates of the British Commonwealth Air Training Plan and personnel of the RAF being posted back to the United Kingdom were used on a one-time basis to fly aircraft.

In the five years of operation, about 100 aircraft were lost with about 300 aircrew both service and civilian. The months of November and December, when weather was at its worst, invariably produced the greatest number of accidents. Considering the circumstances, the ferry service could claim a reasonably good safety record: losses were just over one per cent. *Ferrying Operations – North Atlantic, Second World War*, National Defence, Ottawa.

Prior to joining the family business in Mississippi, **Robert E. Coffman** flew for Colonial Airlines in the four year period following the war. With Mrs. Coffman who was a nurse he met while recuperating from the Greenland experience in Montreal's Royal Victoria Hospital, he lives in Natchez, Mississippi, USA.

Following the war **Norman E. Greenaway** completed his education in Civil Engineering at the University of British Columbia and eventually started his own road construction firm in Saskatoon.

The post-war period saw **Ronald E. Snow** in Argentina for two years where he trained Argentinian air crews and flew DC4s from Buenos Aires to New York, London, and Rome. Then came a career in sales and later, the establishment of his own business. He now resides in Ancaster, Ontario.

Bibliography

Canadian Defence Quarterly, Toronto: Defence Publications, Summer, 1982.

Capon, Alan R. *Mascots of the Hastings and Prince Edward Regiment.* Picton: The Picton Gazette Publishing Company Limited, 1977.

Caulfield, Max. *A Night of Terror: The Story of The* Athenia *Affair.* London: Frederick Muller Ltd., 1958.

Churchill, Winston S. *The Second World War. Volume Three: The Grand Alliance. Volume Four: The Hinge of Fate. Volume Five: Closing The Ring.* London: The Reprint Society, 1953. Cord Cummunications Corporation and Thomas Parrish. *The Simon and Schuster Encyclopedia of World War II.* New York: Simon and Schuster, 1978.

Douglas, W.A.B. and Brereton Greenhous. *Out of The Shadows.* Toronto: Oxford University Press, 1977

Illustrated. London News. 16 September 1939.

Kennedy, J de N. *History of the Department of Munitions and Supply, Canada in the Second World War.* Ottawa: The King's Printer, 1950.

Maclean's. 1 March 1944

Minister of National Defence. *The Canadian Army at War, No. 1. Revised.* The King's Printer, 1946.

Nicholson, Gerald. *Canada's Nursing Sisters.* Toronto: S. Stevens, Hakkert, 1975.

Penny, Arthur G. *Royal Rifles of Canada, A Short History.* Quebec: to mark the Centenary of the Regiment, (privately printed), 28 February 1962.

Rohwer, Jurger. *Die U-Boat-Erfolge-Der-Achsenmachte* 1939-1945. Munich: J. F. Lehmanns Verlag, 1968.

Ruffee, Lieut. G.E.M. and L/Bdr. J. B. Dickie. *The History of the 14th Field Regiment, Royal Canadian Artillery 1940-1945.* Amsterdam: Wereldbibliotheek N.V., September 1945. Stacey, C.P. Arms, *Men and Governments; the war policies of Canada, 1939-45.* Ottawa: Queen's Printer, 1970.

Smith, Kenneth B. *Duffy's Regiment.* Don Mills: T. H. Best Printing Company Ltd., 1983.

The Daily Telegraph and Morning Post. London: 5 September 1939.

The Evening News. London: 4 September 1939, 15 January 1946.
     Thomas, David A. *Japan's War at Sea, Pearl Harbour to the Coral Sea.* London: Andre Deutsch, 1978.

Wade, Mason. *The French Canadians, 1760-1945.* London: Macmillan, 1945.

Acknowledgements

To each of the persons featured in this book who so generously related their World War II experiences and lent appropriate photographs, the author extends sincere thanks. Joyce Hibbert also extends her appreciation to other individuals and organizations whose help made the compilation of this book an easier task.

Dr. Margaret Allemang PhD.
Mary F. Bailey
Ernest Bieber
Captain R. D. Bradford, Unit Information Officer, Hastings and
    Prince Edward Regiment
Kathleen (Kay) Christie
Jane Dewar, Editor, *Legion* magazine
Margaret M. Doull
Ferry Command Association, Montreal. Lillian Wheeler, Publicity
    and Membership
Geodaetisk Institut, Copenhagen, Denmark
Nadine J. Gordon
Gordon Gow
Imperial War Museum, London, England. Terence C. Charman,
    Department of Printed Books, E.C. Hine, Department of
    Photographs
Lydia Oorthuys-Krienen, foto archief Cas Oorthuys, Amsterdam,
    Holland
Merchant Navy Association, Montreal. Bill Riddell.
Alice Morin
Farley Mowat
National Defence Headquarters, Ottawa, W.A. MacIntosh
Netherlands State Institute For War Documentation, Amsterdam,
    Holland
Office de Tourisme, Dieppe, France
Office of the Air, Military and Naval Attache, Italian Embassy,
    Ottawa
Office of the Consulate General of the Netherlands, Montreal
Office of the Royal Danish Embassy, Ottawa
Public Archives Canada. Michel Gauvin, Archivist, Manuscript
    Division, Joy Houston, National Photography Collection, I.
    Légère, The Library, Barbara Wilson, State and Military Records
RAF Museum, Hendon, England. Sebastian Cox M.A., Department
    of Printed Books
Audrie Richards
Royal Canadian Legion, Branch 62, Sarnia, Ontario
Saskatchewan War Brides Association, Kay Garside, Secretary-
    Treasurer
Samuel F. Short
Mary Thomas
Transport Canada, Ottawa
Eileen Walker

Photograph Credits

Front cover: In Hamburg, April 1945, Georgie Rideout (left), a Canadian Army doctor and Lieutenant Nursing Sister Elma Copeland of Field Dressing Station No. 6. Courtesy of Georgie Rideout Seeley.

Back Cover: DND/Public Archives Canada/Pa-128193
Nursing Sisters of No. 10 Canadian General Hospital, RCAMC, landing at Arromanches, France, 23 July 1944.

Public Archives Canada/PA-116533
Troops of the Nova Scotia Highlanders and the Highland Light Infantry of Canada landing at Bernières-sur-Mer, France 6 June 1944.

About the Author

Joyce Hibbert's ongoing interest in World War II began with her own participation in it. As a young woman of seventeen, she joined the Women's Auxiliary Air Force serving with the Royal Observer Corps. Stationed at Horsham Centre, Sussex, England, she was first a plotter, then a spotter at outdoor post L4 at Peacehaven.

After the war, she married her Canadian fiancé, Eric, and moved to Drummondville, Quebec where she raised a family and developed her interest in writing. She has written for newspapers and magazines. An active member of the War Brides Association, she wrote *The War Brides* (PMA, 1978; NAL, 1980).